THE SACRED ART OF CAREGIVING

A Practical Guide to Caring for the Elderly

The author, a professional caregiver, shares compassionate advice and strategies to those who work with the elderly, which will assist them in gaining or improving their caregiving skills. And, more specifically, he offers information which will help them maintain their health and sanity while doing so.

BY

James W. Ramage, MSW, Ph.D.

Psychotherapist
Consultant in Gerontology

authorHOUSE®

AuthorHouse™
1663 Liberty Drive
Bloomington, IN 47403
www.authorhouse.com
Phone: 1-800-839-8640

Published by AuthorHouse 5/24/2012

ISBN: 978-1-4685-7677-1 (e)
ISBN: 978-1-4685-7678-8 (sc)

Library of Congress Control Number: 2012906364

"A book dedicated to helping the Caregiver
survive, heal and grow."

A CAREGIVER'S PERSPECTIVE

A part of coming of age as a caregiver is acknowledging how our choices narrow over time and how they change. Over the years, as caregivers, what we do with our time and energies opens some doors and closes others as we grow and mature in our roles as caregivers. We do not have to be perfect to be helpful, to gradually make our careers as caregivers have substance, meaning, and relevance. Maybe we will never achieve our initial goals and objectives, but what we do achieve is special. At times, our caregiving work can become overwhelming. It is often even physical. However, it really does not matter because it feels real. We are what we do and should do what we enjoy—caring.

This is the heart and soul of a caregiver.

DISCLAIMER

This book is not a substitute for personal, medical, psychiatric, or psychological diagnosis or treatment. The purpose of the author is to offer educational information to individuals who are engaged in the care of the elderly. The information contained in this book does not constitute medical advice, treatment or specific prescriptions. Medical and psychological diagnosis can only occur between an individual patient and their physician or mental health professional.

DEDICATION

This book and its contents are dedicated to my early mentors. First, to my Mother, Florence Westmoreland Ramage, who shared her caregiving skills with me which she practiced most of her life until her death. Second, to my Father, James Thomas Henderson Ramage, also deceased, who taught me to view the world through a different set of eyes. Thirdly, to my wife's parents, Hunter Dewey Moore, deceased, who was one of the finest lay counselors that I have ever known as he listened to and encouraged the many disturbed veterans and others who came by daily to his country store to talk about life and their issues with the military. Also, to his wife, Davie Hudson Moore, now deceased, who provided me with love, encouragement and motivation as the foundation for the birthing of this book. In addition, my sincere appreciation is extended to Mr. Doyce B. Ward, MSW, LCSW, retired, who was my first professional mentor who taught me the fundamentals of caregiving.

HOPE

A Hidden Ingredient of Caregiving

Hope is an important and vital element of caregiving. This fragile emotional response is a human trait. It is an essential and necessary resource to life. If denied or suppressed, the human body and mind becomes sick – affecting all dimensions of the human being – physically, mentally, emotionally and spiritually. Hope is food for the soul and security for the spirit. If hope is replaced by despair, it robs a person of their stability, which prevents them from being at peace with others, with their God, and with themselves. Hope makes their life enjoyable resulting in their savoring existence itself. Hope revives thoughts and memories of one's youth, which are embedded deep within their psychic that has a gravitational pull towards spiritual wellness. The art of caregiving should encompass the idea of giving encouragement, of maintaining a sympathetic ear, and to give a warm hug to those who are old, frail, and tired especially those who have a terminal illness. Their hope, although at times futile, is to be embraced rather than being discouraged. Hope is and always will be a secret weapon in caregiving. This hidden ingredient is a significant element in caregiving and is essential in any prescription of care and wellness.

CONTENTS

INTRODUCTION

Although caregiving is as old as human kind there has been considerable progress in addressing itself to key issues in the healthcare profession. Perhaps the most progress made over the years has been the acceptance and realization by other professional disciplines and the general public that caregiving is a vital part of living, that it is a legitimate, recognized and accepted profession.

I am often asked why would anyone choose or volunteer to be a caregiver. Why would anyone want to spend their careers in situations that would drive other people nuts? Why would a man or woman enter families just as the family members are running and clawing their way for the exit? Why would one want to intervene in facing out-of-control chaos? Why do they think that they can bring peace, understanding and sanity to replace violence, warfare and every form of craziness known to man? Is it because we are fierce folks and it takes a lot of crazy demands and behavior to scare us.

Although many of us may experience some or all of those concerns, those of us who have made caregiving a career have done so because we care. We do so because we possess as human beings, most if not all, of the gifts of the spirit such as service, humbleness, humility, forgiveness, creativity, clarity and love. We are caregivers because we live with a purpose, fully whole, empowered and inwardly secure. We perform duties as a caregiver out of gratitude believing that the soul should be cared for as well as our physical body. These values are the true meaning of the "Sacred Art of Caregiving" to which we adhere.

During my career as a caregiver I have logged somewhere in the neighborhood of something over 60,000 hours working with the elderly, their families, and other caregivers who were "worn out", "tired of being tired", laboring with residents around the clock without reserving any time for themselves. I have somehow managed to remain reasonably sane and healthy during the process. I have helped most of the individuals with whom I have provided services and have surely disappointed some. After all this time, I still approach each day eagerly and optimistically and do not feel burned out or bored, at least not for very long periods of time. It is still fun, an honor, and a great satisfaction to see someone respond in a positive manner after having been in need and hurting. Moreover, it has to be fun, because I could not survive with those unfortunate people who are old, frail, and have a terminal illness without taking care of my own mental and physical needs.

The purpose of this book is to help individuals who are serving, or who are considering becoming a caregiver for the elderly. It concerns itself primarily with the relationships between people and the attitudes that are the essential therapeutic skills, which are employed by those of us who work as caregivers. While we as caregivers are in the most constant contact with the elderly resident and, therefore, most directly concerned with the older resident, their illness, welfare and environment, there are others working with the resident and their families who will find the same material helpful.

The book will also be useful to students in the field of Human Services who assist the elderly in their homes, assisted living and long-term care facilities. I believe that relatives of the elderly will benefit by reading the contents of this book and will be encouraged that better care of their older relative or significant other is assured when the material in this book is applied during their period of habilitation, care or end of life issues.

CHAPTER ONE

THE EVOLVING PROCESS OF CAREGIVING

I wrote this book because I had a need as a caregiver to help those who are struggling to provide basic hands-on care to the elderly. The core values of my profession and background from which I come dictated that I do so. Then, in addition, I did so because I love what I do, respect and admire the riveting intensity of the countless number of caregivers with whom I have had the privilege of counseling over the years, both individually and in group therapy. My enduring frustration has been my inability to convince this group of caregivers who perform the basic elements of caregiving, of their worth, value and contributions they make to the healthcare industry.

This group of caregivers are individuals who I genuinely like. They do an outstanding job providing services, which are at times extremely discouraging, heartbreaking and beyond the call of duty. They do their jobs well with little, if any, formal education. I do so because of the extremely personal nature of care those caregivers provide to the elderly residents for whom they are caring. Although these caregivers have exceedingly difficult jobs, most bond with the resident, over time, providing support, gaining greater wisdom and compassion for their residents. Therefore, they are in a position to contribute important and vital information, which is usually unknown to other staff members when formulating goals, objectives and strategies to assist with their care and at times behavior problems. Their motivation is usually stated on their applications for employment as "because I like to care for old folks" or "I know I can work with the elderly because I have cared for my Grandmother who is old and bedfast for years." In reality, they have little experience or knowledge of the elderly and their physiological, sociological, and psychological backgrounds that is required of us who are professional caregivers in healthcare and other fields of study. Furthermore, they have limited knowledge of the habilitation potential of a resident, which is vital for developing an adequate care plan and the implications of a particular diagnosis. All this and more has to be learned from the professional staff in never-ending in-service training sessions and constant supervision.

Many of these men and women who labor as caregivers are long-suffering, taking a great deal of verbal abuse. There always seems to be those on the staff who feel that these individuals are employed to do whatever they want done regardless of whether it is needed or not. Some feel that they are going to get their money's worth by making demands of this group of caregivers, which go far beyond what is in their job descriptions. Others are just outright disrespectful. This group seems to always bear the blunt of some of the staff and their life-long frustrations.

Over the years of counseling, I analyzed many of the reasons why this group of caregivers feels so insecure in their jobs and the reasons why so many with good potential leave their place of employment and move on. As stated previously, they enter the healthcare industry handicapped by a lack of adequate formal education and training. In addition, the professional community is not always receptive and understanding. As a result they enter the workplace with mixed feelings of insecurity, inadequacy, and of being ill prepared to function in a position in which they feel unqualified and much less of being able of contributing to the treatment and care of another human being. Many are never able to accept and outgrow their feelings of fear and inferiority. When performing their duties they recall previous jobs they have held. For example, they remember their work as a homemaker, mother, father, farmer, seamstress, sales person, or even a bartender. Others recalled their experiences and feelings of inadequacy in their roles of child rearing and the many problems they encountered during the process, questioning their parenting skills.

Now that they were beginning a new venture in their lives in healthcare, they brought these old fears with them. These fears were further inflamed when the nursing supervisor that interviewed them for a position as caregiver wanted to know about their education, experience, work history and their reason for wanting to work as a caregiver. This resulted in their having ambivalent feelings and undue anxieties regarding the many issues which they would face. They worried about having to deal with inappropriate behavior, physical, mental, spiritual and emotional needs of the resident, including the issues of end of life. In addition, they often feel intimidated by the thought of working with such important well-educated professionals, which frightened and overwhelmed them further contributing to their feelings of low self-esteem.

One of the quickest and most effective ways that we can gain self-confidence, feel needed, accepted and a part of the staff is to attend interdisciplinary team meetings. We as a member of the direct care staff are an essential part of the team. We are the one member who will be attending who knows more about the resident than anyone else does. Our contributions are vital. Our input is valued and important to the holistic care of the resident. It is here that we will have the opportunity to meet and get to know the various members of the staff with whom we will be working.

At the heart of the concept of interdisciplinary teamwork is the joining of dissimilar caregiver skills to attack different aspects of a common problem. In successful team practice, relationships that cross disciplinary boundaries may be very close, and each caregiver is concerned with facilitating the achievement of all the participants. Smooth communication bridges the gap between the thinking of one caregiver and the useful ideas of colleagues. The team approach gives each participant an opportunity to develop and expand relationships and change our professional frame of reference. It is perhaps the quickest way to get to know our colleagues, put us at ease, reduce our anxieties and improve our knowledge base thus giving us a sense of confidence, respect, and reassures us that our input is important to insuring holistic care for the resident. We also think about our responsibilities to our families and wonder if our relationships with them would change, or would it blend, have substance, meaning and relevance.

During my counseling sessions with these individuals, I always placed emphasis on what they already knew. For example, as adults they had faced the trials and tribulations of life as it had come at them---the good, the bad and the ugly. In addition, I have always tried to impress upon them that caring for the elderly is much like caring for children during the formative years. It has been my experience that if an adult is good at parenting they generally make good caregivers, especially for the older resident with dementia or Alzheimer's disease. I make every effort to impress on them that becoming a quality caregiver requires basic strategies. They

4

are: 1) never bring a personal or family issue to work. Residents are extremely sensitive to mood disorders, inappropriate mental, emotional or unresolved behavior problems on the part of the caregiver. 2) Get to know the resident – his or her name and what they prefer to be called; their habits in relation to life's basic needs such as eating, bathing, dressing, sleeping, elimination, medications, and outstanding reasons for their inappropriate behavior. 3) understand the resident so that the reasons for certain inappropriate behavior patterns become clear and so that the knowledge of these reasons can be used constructively during the process of care. 4) Develop good communication skills with the resident and his or her family. It is of paramount importance that the caregivers are aware of themselves in terms of the effect that the resident has on them as a caregiver and that the caregiver be aware of how they are affecting the resident. This is important because the caregiver is the one person who maintains constant interaction with the resident for sustained lengths of time. Therefore, it is the caregiver upon whom the resident depends for a secure environment and proper care.

Physical care brings to mind the tangible aspects of the duties of the caregiver at home or in a nursing home setting. They are concerned with the resident's activities of daily living. The caregiver must know if and how the resident sleeps, eats, drinks, and makes sure that the resident is properly toileted, bathed, groomed and dressed. Then, there are housekeeping duties, keeping the living environment of the resident healthy. In addition, they must know the elementary signs and symptoms of physical illnesses in addition to having some knowledge of mental and emotional disorders and report them quickly and accurately to appropriate professional staff. Also, they must be familiar with the more commonly used interactive drugs, and, be particularly alert to the undesirable side effects. Moreover, in addition, they must be able to make beds appropriately, assist with special treatments, make routine checks of equipment and laundry, keep accurate count of his or her residents, weigh them, and a dozen other errands, all of which are important to the health, safety and welfare of the resident for whom they are responsible.

In all these tasks, they must learn to respect their co-workers. They must work with them to help the nurses in the performance of their duties to keep the physician informed about their resident's health. Then, in addition, they must aid in the work being done by other caregivers and continue their diversional activity at home or long-term care facilities.

There are all kinds of emergencies in which they have to also participate. They may be required to stay with a resident who is exhibiting inappropriate behavior, or help transport a resident from one area to another, to the hospital or clinic. In many instances, they may have to accompany the social worker in escorting a resident to the hospital or physician. In some instances, they help count and sort laundry or are responsible for the residents' clothing and valuables, or assist with meals. Whatever the assignment the caregiver will do well to develop a healthy philosophy about their work and use accumulated knowledge as their primary guide in caring for a resident or residents in their care.

Up until Federal Law 42 CRF 483.15 was passed, the screening process for hiring personnel to fill nursing assistant positions, then known as aids or orderlies, amounted to little or nothing. Knowledge of leadership, work ethics, and quality of care resulted in far too many instances to neglect and abuse. There was little emphasis placed on background checks which frequently resulted in petty criminals, alcoholics, neurotics, character disorders and shiftless individuals going to work in a nursing home setting because no place else would consider them for employment; or because the facility needed help so desperately that anyone who could walk and talk was better than nothing. Because of federal intervention, nursing homes now require that all skilled nursing home facilities provide medical services to attain or maintain the resident's highest practicable physical, mental, and psychosocial care. As a result, nursing homes are placing greater emphasis on hiring competent personnel to fill assistants' positions. It also places emphasis on our educational systems to do more in training a professional work force of men and women to work in the healthcare industry and more specifically in nursing homes as Certified Nursing Assistants. These individuals should possess certain characteristics and attributes such as humane principles, an interest in being of service to their fellowman, recognize a person's condition as sickness, and want to do something about it. There should be more impetus placed on education for the nursing assistant. At least six (6) months of classroom instruction should be required to address the physiological, sociological and psychological aspects of human growth and development in an undergraduate program in college and some clinical experience in working with the elderly.

With improved conditions in today's nursing home industry, the nursing assistant serving as a caregiver still falls into five main categories when applying for a position as a caregiver. They are as follows: 1) The person who has tried many jobs and/or vocations and feels that a job as a nursing assistant in a nursing home caring for the elderly will offer security, interest and will put them in a position to make a contribution to the community. 2) A homemaker who needs a job to provide a second income to assist her spouse in maintaining the family. 3) The student who needs work while going to school or desires to gain experience, which will offer them better preparation for their chosen career in the health field. 4) The "drifter", who is of the opinion that the nursing home environment is a "soft touch" for a while, or feels protected in an environment of sick people, or is domineering enough to want to work where they can assert themselves with people who, for the most part, cannot or will not defend themselves or their rights. The term "drifter" is used here because, fortunately, those who fall into this category are becoming fewer and far between and are the ones who are not dependable, who do not accept their share of the work responsibilities, who are always late or absent from work and are responsible for many of the accidents, falls, and abuse which happen to the elderly. 5) The person who wishes to make a career of being a nursing assistant, who starts out with this in mind and pursues every opportunity to prepare him or herself for the position or a better one.

In order to take care of the elderly, one should always keep in mind that the resident is usually sick, suffering from a physical, mental, emotional disorder, or dementia accompanied by inappropriate behavior. They do so even though they may seem to know when they are exhibiting unacceptable behavior. The fact is that they do so, even though it is quite clear that the desire of those around them is to be of help, indicates that they are sick. The resident is a person who at times loses control, who becomes not only depressed but also very depressed, who at times becomes not only angry but also very angry. The resident is often sick because they have lost faith in those persons who are closest to them. They feel that they are alone, have no one who cares or someone to lean on. They need someone who cares, someone who cares about what happens to them, someone who can talk with them, someone who can teach them the activities of daily living. They need to know and to be with another human being who will accept and help them adjust to the facility. It is this recognition of the resident's illness and their inherent needs that must be constantly kept uppermost in the mind of the nursing assistant in the performance of their duties as a caregiver.

Regardless of one's education, profession, or position in life, we are all caregivers at one time or another during our lifetime. Some of us become caregivers by choice while others become caregivers out of necessity. Before committing oneself to caregiving, one should give serious thought to the responsibilities of the job and the emotional stress of caregiving. Because of those demands of the caregiving process, it is recommended that anyone considering becoming a caregiver examine their motivations for doing so. If one decides to accept this awesome responsibility, one should then assess him/herself through introspection to see if they are capable of realistically interacting with the resident in the following manner.

- Listen carefully and attentively to the resident without being defensive or attacking.
- Be observant noticing the resident's appearance, posture, eye contact and tone of voice.
- Be careful never to bombard the resident with direct questions.
- Communicate with the resident to try to understand their thoughts, feelings and meaning.
- Paraphrase communication in your own way as a means of checking and clarifying the content of what is being said and the feelings behind it.

- Use minimal responses like "yes, sir"; "no, ma'am"; nodding, etc. to demonstrate attention, following verbal communication and to encourage further exploration.
- Summarize conversation after the resident has talked for a while picking up clues which will help in their habilitation.
- Use information obtained to address both old and new issues.
- Refrain from accusing or humiliating the resident out of revenge.

If you are considering becoming a caregiver by choice or out of necessity, you should seriously examine your feelings, situation and demands of the job. Having primary responsibility for the health and welfare of another person can be gratifying and rewarding. However, it can also be a difficult, demanding and terrifying experience. This is especially true when caring for an elderly person who also has dementia accompanied with mental, emotional, inappropriate behavior and skill loss. It often becomes a juggling act trying to balance the complex issues and needs of the person for whom we are caring, and maintaining a quality life style with our family and friends. Caregivers are many times, as a result, the invisible laborers without whom neither the health care system nor the frail and elderly person could survive. One should be aware that there are three types of caregivers: 1) those who provide care, 2) those that care, and 3) those that both care and provide care with the latter being the type we all strive to become. However, this is not an easy task to accomplish. Emotional devastation often accompanies the elderly resident who has Alzheimer's dementia, not only for the resident but for the caregiver as well. The caregivers who are forced to watch a resident slowly deteriorate often experience intense periods of emotional turmoil that may be more intense than experienced by a resident's physical death.

Because of this mental and emotional strain, which often results in physical exhaustion, it is crucial that as caregivers we must take care of our own physical and mental health. Our sense of loss often results in depression leaving us feeling helpless and useless. It is here that we often become part of the problem rather than being part of the solution. It often results in our feelings to degenerate to apathy, listlessness, or irritability and even to a reduction of our physical and mental stamina. The beauty, however, of caregiving should be its precision. It means exactly what it says without discrimination.

A significant indication of the sophistication of a society is measured by the attention given to its social issues. One major social problem with which every civilization including this one has struggled is how to address the multi-dimensional needs of its elderly. Previous generations dealt with caring for the elderly with methods, which were quite primitive ranging from abandonment, to persecution, to viewing them as being "crazy". More recently, many were kept isolated in a back room or spent their older years in mental institutions where they received electric shock treatments, or a lobotomy. In addition, they most certainly would have been written off as not having any potential of contributing to society. They would have spent their final years in isolation and shame.

However, then as now, caregivers were present and were active participants in trying to improve conditions for the elderly. Growing out of those harsh conditions came homes for the poor, old folks and county homes, which provided minimal resources to meet their basic needs of food, clothing, and shelter. In those days, individuals dreaded having to face old age – of having to deal with what they called "old timer's disease", a condition they did not understand or comprehend which is now known as Alzheimer's Dementia.

Despite the sophisticated treatment methods, availability of trained personnel and vastly improved educational opportunities misconception about old age, dementia and Alzheimer's disease still exist. If you have an elderly parent, many of these old stigmas most likely continue to lurk somewhere – if not in them, then in you or some other family member or relative. Helping your grandparents or perhaps your parents realize that they should not feel shame over these disorders is one of the most important and vital roles we can play.

We can also play an important role in assisting them to identify and understand the symptoms that signal the existence of dementia disorders especially Alzheimer's disease. It is vital that we convince an aging parent or grandparent that evaluation and treatment should be pursued. It is important that we maintain a supportive and informed relationship with them. Moreover, in doing so our persistence will greatly influence and increase the likelihood that our elderly relatives will ultimately accept professional help which he or she needs.

In comparison to many other health related occupations, the art of caregiving is as old as civilization itself. Caregiving is an action-oriented movement with a heritage which is centuries old. As it has emerged from its youthful period of exuberance into a more sedate and rational maturity, it has managed to retain a high level of spontaneity and flexibility. More importantly, it has kept its boundaries open to facilitate a healthy cross-fertilization of ideas and concepts generated from within as well as from other disciplines which include both professionally trained personnel as well as the untrained volunteer. Caregiving is regarded as a strength by some and a weakness by others in that the movement has consciously resisted delimiting definitions that it has taken. This course of action grew out of an apprehension that such forays into semantically entanglements would only result in premature closure of intellectual stagnation – a condition that affects many of the other health disciplines in today's society

While an attitude of openness and individual determinism is a highly cherished commodity in the movement of caregiving, it has contributed to a level of diversity, which makes it impossible for any individual to fully comprehend, much less speak for, the movement as a whole. Regardless of this heterogeneity, the caregiving movement is bound by a credo, which is firmly implanted in all who would presume to identify with the movement. This credo affirms the belief that all individuals, especially the elderly, regardless of their disabling condition are entitled to equal opportunities for the best healthcare available. To this end, caregiving is and should always be aimed at providing meaningful training opportunities to improve and provide care for the elderly, ill, disabled, handicapped and otherwise socio culturally disadvantaged whenever and wherever their services are needed.

The Certified Nursing Assistant constitutes the largest group of caregivers contributing to the care of the elderly. Most are employed by the nursing home industry, hospices, assisted living, long-term care facilities, and units designed to provide special care for individuals suffering from Alzheimer's disease and other dementias. With the exploding population of the nation's elderly and sudden mushrooming of extended care facilities and other types of homes for the elderly, more and better-trained caregivers are needed. Advancements in the care and treatment of the elderly have and are occurring so rapidly that it is imperative to revise current thinking, attitudes, and philosophy towards the recruitment and training of the caregiver. In reflecting on the continued seriousness of illnesses in the elderly especially Alzheimer's disease, and other types of dementia are primary health problems. It remains essentially true that humane kindness, consistent relationships and perceptive understanding are still and will remain the basic ingredients in caring for the elderly suffering from dementia.

The ever-baffling illnesses with which the caregiver has to cope in the elderly are those who are often frail, seriously ill, confused and demented. They are over eighty years old with major skill loss, which requires constant and extended care. In addition, many have severe psychological problems. They are unstable, depressed, and often suffering from dementia, in addition to, mood and bipolar disorders and at times even with schizophrenia accompanied by inappropriate behavior, which further complicates the caregiver's ability to provide appropriate and quality care. It is tragic that training that is more formal has not been made available to the caregiving community. This is unusual when one considers that the basic care of the elderly is largely their responsibility. This trend will likely continue well into the future since the medical staff and other professional caregivers who work with the elderly in our extended care facilities are so overwhelmed by the needs and demands of the elderly and their families. They cannot begin to care for their elderly residents without the assistance of volunteers and the Certified Nursing Assistants who provide caregiving services.

Caregivers face a multitude of problems while they perform their duties, which are often complex in the residents home and healthcare facilities. Currently caregivers are faced with the following issues as they struggle in their efforts to maintain a sense of normalcy and balance in trying to meet the needs of their family, their personal interests and at the same time provide quality services for the resident for whom they are caring. Their caregiving duties seem to never end especially if they are a woman. Other issues, which complicate the role of the caregiver, are:

- A demand for more sophiscated attention and care.
- An increasing dependency upon the caregiver to be more productive.
- To provide care for a larger population of the elderly with declining cognitive skills.
- To serve a larger population of elderly residents with catastrophic illnesses.
- To tolerate more physical violence and verbal abuse.
- To experience more communication problems.
- To resist looking at themselves through introspection.
- Have a limited knowledge of theories behind the behavior of the elderly.
- Experience neglect of their own physical and emotional needs.

The most unique contribution, which is made by the caregiver, is his or her complicated and sometimes complex job of caring for the elderly especially those who have Alzheimer's dementia with associated behavior problems. How effective he or she is in caring for the elderly is his or her closeness to the person for whom services are being provided. The hard work and the faithfulness of the caregiver are and will remain the mainstay of all the facilities, including home care, in this nation.

Not all caregivers fulfill this description, but the majority of them do. It is the opinion of the author that there is no doubt that the future holds a prominent recognition for the caregiver, which is so rightfully his or hers. Perhaps we will never achieve our initial goals and objectives as a caregiver, but what we do and how we do it is special. At times, our caregiving work can and does tax our emotions both mentally and physically, but it is satisfying because it feels real. We are what we are. We do what we do. However, in the end, we will die anyway but then that is all right as well because that is life...

CHAPTER TWO

THE IMPORTANCE OF ATTITUDE

Those of us who serve as caregivers should always take our responsibilities seriously. We should have a sincere desire to help the elderly person for whom we are caring. As a caregiver, our behavior should be professional at all times. Our mission should be to assist the resident to improve and maintain his or her skill level, activities of daily living, their self-esteem, and give them hope. Therefore, our attitude during the caregiving process is of paramount importance. Our attitude is even more important when the individual for whom we are caring has dementia or Alzheimer's disease.

In considering the problem of healthful and non-healthful attitudes, we must consider not only current attitudes of the public, but also our attitude as a caregiver. It is relatively simple to tell us how to do it. The how of doing things involves most emphatically the personality of the individual performing the task. Every personality is different, just as every person is different. How we affect others in our interaction with them and how others affect us involves many components of us, which make up a total picture of our personality.

There are many available definitions of the personality. In

fact, entire books have been written to address the subject. If we consider an everyday evaluation of the meaning of personality, it involves the physical, mental and spiritual aspects of an individual – their development in relation to the social sphere in which one lives. Their appearance, voice, mannerisms, control, general intelligence, ability and warmth are the main ingredients of the over-all personality. Warmth should especially be considered, since it involves efforts to move one towards others with understanding and with sympathy, exhibiting humor and relatedness. We judge another's personality quite simply by the way in which he or she affects us. For example, a limp handshake can discourage respect rapidly, and a loud, boisterous voice may arouse feelings of anger toward the caregiver. A clean, neat appearance attracts compliments and attention whereas a soiled and unkept appearance, though it assuredly attracts attention, arouses critical comments and negative opinions. The resident who laughs too easily and too much, or becomes angry too quickly is viewed with some degree of anxiety by his or her peers as well as the caregiver.

We as caregivers, whether or not we are aware of it, use our personality as the first and most important tool in dealing with the resident for whom we are caring. Our ability to size up the personality of the resident is a secondary, but also an important, tool. Thus, it will be emphasized, repeatedly by the author that knowing the resident and the important expressions of his or her behavior is the first task of the caregiver. Not only is it important to know a resident and what to expect of them in terms of behavior but also to understand and comprehend one's own feelings about such behavior. This, of course, involves forming an attitude.

In earlier generations, as previously mentioned in the preceding chapter, people dealt with the elderly in different ways and means.

Most unfortunately, some punished and ridiculed the elderly while most were concerned with getting rid of them – out of sight – out of mind. The basis for such an attitude was out of fear or ignorance. They did not know the why and wherefore of conditions like Alzheimer's disease and other dementias blaming old age and was afraid of growing old because of what they called "old timer's disease". Today, such attitudes still prevail but are not addressed in the same drastic manner as in the past. As we grow and move more toward an urban way of life, the tendency is still to "get rid of" the elderly, since we cannot let a resident wander the streets or community or tolerate their inappropriate behavior. Unacceptable behavior can and is tolerated more if an elderly person who has Alzheimer's disease resides on a farm or a rural area. It is when they bring their behaviors to town that usually results in institutionalization in a nursing home or long-term care facility. People still view Alzheimer's disease and the inappropriate behavior associated with the disease as unacceptable viewing them as being "crazy", "loonies", or "nuts" and continue to look to psychiatric facilities to provide care for them. Although this is beginning to change, it is and will continue to be a slow process. The trend in today's society points toward aggressive research for a cure for Alzheimer's disease and other types of dementia. In addition, modern facilities and treatment strategies are being designed specifically to address dementia and more specifically Alzheimer's disease.

It is not unusual for many in today's society to express their concern for those of us who work with the elderly as caregivers especially those residents who have behavior problems. Some worry about caregivers, especially if they happen to be a female. They worry about her being physically assaulted. Although this primary attitude cannot be condoned, yet neither can it be criticized. It is the direct result of a lack of knowledge about the elderly and their medical, psychosocial, psychological and spiritual needs. Spending time with residents under the supervision of a competent, experienced caregiver will dispel most if not all of such fears and attitudes more quickly than will educational classes and self-help books. The elderly residents are, first, people, and they are people in need of help. An elderly resident who is frail, and sick especially those with dementia or Alzheimer's disease, is usually sensitive and to some degree has awareness of the feelings of those around him or her. This sensitivity makes it necessary for the caregiver to develop and maintain healthful attitudes. Some of the attitudes and emotional issues the caregiver will need to be familiar with are:

SYMPATHY AND EMPATHY

What kinds of attitude are the most productive as a basis for successful relationships with residents? Feelings of superiority, authority, ridicule and a physical overpowering attitude must be weeded out. In place of them, sympathy can be substituted – not an emotional gush of pity, but a sincere, humble kind of sympathy that recognizes that dementia knows no selection. In other words, "there, but for the Grace of God, go I". A seasoned caregiver once told me and I have heard similar comments since, "working with old people for me is God's Work. I often think as I bathe them, help feed and toilet them, that it might well be my own Mother, Father, or Grandparents that I am caring for, and I find my work, as difficult as it is, to be patient because of that thought." A caregiver cannot hear a resident cry without feeling some of the pain, mental, and emotional anguish behind the cry.

Empathy is another important attitude, which is not so easily achieved. As is sympathy, a caregiver has to experience feelings as well as responses in order to empathize. For example, a caregiver who is a wife and mother can share her experience of labor and childbirth with a resident who has been a mother and grandmother. A caregiver who has brought his or her alcoholism or drug addition under control can give much to the alcoholic or drug addict. A caregiver who has been divorced by a wife or husband may well be more aware of the anguish the rejected resident feels.

Fortunately, we can usually work through these periods of uncontrolled emotions without professional help and keeping emotions under control when caring for our residents. Maybe a friend, spouse or co-worker can lend some support, but mostly we as caregivers must learn to become aware of our stress and emotional difficulties, it's cause and attempt to eliminate it. We have to learn to take care of ourselves so that we can function as a caregiver adequately at work and at home.

The elderly resident is in a nursing home or receiving care because he or she is old, frail and sick with possible dementia or a psychiatric disorder. As a result, our residents face new environments, situations, and as a result are going to experience certain emotional responses. As a caregiver, we must be aware of what these responses are likely to be, since more often than not, their responses will be exaggerated, and the resident will need help in coping with them.

FEAR

The most common basic emotional response to the needs of residents fall into five basic categories: 1) fear, 2) anger, 3) grief,

4), hate and 5) love. It is important for caregivers to have some knowledge of these basic human emotional traits, which all humans possess. It is not by chance that fear is the first of these emotions to be listed. Fear is the emotion, which is always present for the elderly resident especially those who suffer from Alzheimer's dementia. This holds true because fear is an element, which conditions most of the resident's activities and the activities of those around him or her. The resident may be afraid of being separated from their loved ones.

Actually, most of us as caregivers, at one time or another, experience some of the mental and emotional turmoil with which residents cannot cope. This could very well account for that immeasurable quality of "heart" that some of us as caregivers have toward the elderly resident. It stems from life's experiences, which is not acquired in formal classroom study.

It is possible to remain somewhat detached when the feeling is that of sympathy. On the other hand, empathy is more involved because we as caregivers know how the elderly resident feels if we have been there and done that. However, as with sympathy, empathy can be overdone and, therefore, not be healthy for either the resident or caregiver. An examination of attitudes is as follows:

HOPEFULNESS

For the caregiver an attitude of hope is essential. One of the greatest dangers for us as caregivers must guard against is allowing ourselves to reach a point of despair about the lack of progress our resident is making. This is sometimes extremely difficult, for no illness is more baffling and discouraging than dementia or Alzheimer's disease. A feeling of defeat is very quickly communicated to the resident, and when the resident loses hope, the battle for life diminishes. The chances for his or her maintaining skills at their present level slide further down the scale. Each year new methods and strategies are studied for the treatment of Alzheimer's and other types of dementia. It should be remembered that hope is always the secret weapon of the caregiver.

KINDNESS

As caregivers, we should appreciate the fact that gentleness and courtesy indicates an attitude of kindness. Most residents being cared for by us are sick of suffering from a physical, mental, emotional, or psychological disorder. Many have difficulty relating to people in general and have as a result become victims of society, which has resulted in low-self esteem, a defeatist attitude and depression. We as a caregiver, substituting for a family member or friend, can restore the resident's self-respect by our thoughtfulness. Such thoughtfulness should be a part of everyday activities and interaction with the resident. All residents want to love and to be loved. When a resident feels loved, it is not difficult for us to be kind and considerate. When the resident is disliked or constantly irritated, it becomes a matter of controlling the feelings of dislike and perhaps even changing it by taking more time to be gentle and courteous when lifting, turning, dressing, feeding, toileting or talking with the resident. This involves the development of our patience. Patience is an art, which means a sincere effort toward understanding behavior. Losing patience with an elderly resident who is ill such as yelling, pushing, a lack of verbal and physical interaction, withholding emotional involvement with him or her is never acceptable or excusable. Not only is it inexcusable, it is abuse.

In addition, it can undo, in a very short period, any good, which has been accomplished by us after days of hard work.

REALISM

An attitude of realism in relation to a resident is an extremely important factor to us as caregivers in the process of assisting, improving, or maintaining his or her skill level. We should not allow ourselves to agree with or support a resident's bizarre ideas or behavior, since this merely strengthens and reinforces such ideas in the resident's mind. However, it does not mean that his or her behavior cannot be tolerated, or ridiculed, since there are times in the course of the resident's illness when it is necessary for the resident to talk or "get out" his or her inner feelings. It is necessary for us to remember, always, that no matter what the resident says or does, no matter how vague, unreasonable or eccentric, it may appear, it means something to the resident and we as caregivers should not over-react but be patient and make every effort to find what the resident's behavior means. As caregivers, we represent to the resident his or her only contact with the real or outside world. Therefore, we should make every attempt at all times, to maintain a realistic attitude towards the resident's needs and to define and build on his or her strengths rather than their weaknesses.

RESPECT

A resident's self-respect is the strength of his or her personality. With it, he or she can face the world and contribute to society and the welfare of humankind. For many reasons the elderly individual, often involves the loss of self-respect. Society places great emphasis on youth. When the elderly are disabled, frail, and sick they often loose their self-esteem. They, in far too many instances, feel unloved and unwanted even by their own families. Not only is it frequently a cause of their illness, but at times it is the result of their illness. The stigma attached to being in a nursing home, a strange environment or room, with a strange person, and loss of their independence is often communicated by thoughtless relatives, employers, and friends and the resident may be ashamed of having to be cared for by someone else. Therefore, it is of the utmost importance for us to rebuild carefully with the resident his or her self-respect, and to gain their confidence and trust, first in us as a caregiver and ultimately in him or herself. We should develop an attitude of respect for the resident as a human being who is unable to care for him or herself. Respect involves such things as appreciating the resident's need for privacy, their need to have possessions they can call their own as well as an emotional need for attention and to be understood.

We should realize that whatever attitudes we develop toward the resident would also be carried into the community at large. There is no end of goodwill toward caring for the elderly, long-term care facilities or home care, which can be built if we as caregivers communicate to his or her own circle of friends and associates sound, healthful attitudes. Such attitudes and communication is good public relations. The rule of us as an "unofficial public relations officer" should be assumed as part of our duties and done by us as quickly as possible, since it is one of the important obligations of the caregiver's job. People may be hesitant toward accepting a healthy viewpoint in exchange for a fearful one. However, as with the theory of water wearing down a stone, every drop counts and every positive word by us in our community is important toward wearing down negative opinions about a nursing home, assisted living, long-term care facility or home care for the elderly in which we are employed.

EMOTIONAL NEEDS

Any discussion of attitudes leads most naturally into a dialogue about emotions. Our emotional status is usually conditioned by the attitudes of those around us, the family, friends, co-workers and acquaintances. Feelings and emotions are so closely related that they mean practically the same thing. However, emotions generally are understood to indicate a stronger response when compared to attitudes. The two terms will be used similarly in discussing the needs of the resident for an understanding of a resident and his or her reactions to people and to things.

EMOTIONAL CONTROL

Almost everyone including caregivers at one time or another, experiences a period of a lack of emotional control. That is, we get very tired and discouraged. There are times we get to the point of becoming so depressed about it that our work, our relationships with our family, and many other interests and responsibilities may suffer. Then in addition, we become irritable looking everywhere for arguments and in general creating an unpleasant atmosphere for others and ourselves.

The resident may fear a new or strange environment, the dark, fellow residents, staff members or loneliness. If admitted to a long-term facility, he or she may fear losing their independence, plus dozens of other things such as death, dying, food, or sharing a room with a stranger in an unfamiliar facility. The resident is faced with all sorts of necessary procedures such as a physical examination, routine bathing, dozens of personal questions, the removal of personal possessions. He or she meets in a short period of time, any number of individuals whom they have never seen before. It does not matter how kind or caring we are, the resident may still feel that we are all eager to do them harm.

There are two general responses to the emotion of fear. First, the resident may lash out in an attempt to eliminate their fear, and, second, they may withdraw. The average resident who withdraws does so by avoiding other residents and personnel, by remaining in his or her room, refusing to eat, or sometimes refusing to cooperate. This pattern of withdrawal, which is the direct result of fear, demands patience on the part of us who is responsible for the resident's well-being. A quite, friendly, and consistent approach to such behavior does two things: 1) It builds the resident's confidence in us as a person, and 2) it can demonstrate to the resident, by example, that they will be free from the harm that is so desperately feared. It is important to remember that this type of reaction to fear on the part of a resident may result from his or her being neglected in the past or feeling neglected by us. As caregivers, we must always be aware that residents often feel neglected in an active home or institutional environment. We must be careful that the resident does not get or feel lost in the rush of mandatory activities occurring in an active busy environment providing care to the elderly.

On the other hand, a resident who reacts to fear by striking out may do so in a number of ways; they may be extremely loud, talkative, noisy, destructive, or even assaultive. The resident may pick on others, keep his or her living area disturbed at night, or refuse to eat, sleep, toilet him or herself, wander about the facility, and generally causing a disturbance. At times, such behavior can be interpreted as being a lifelong habit of being uncooperative, hostile, or stubborn. However, we as caregivers must keep in mind that the resident is old, sick, frail, and many times suffer from a mental or emotional disorder. We can recognize his or her need for reassuring human presence. Try to avoid the use of physical force in dealing with this type of behavior. Make every effort in this case to be patient, kind, understanding and reassuring. This instills trust, upon which the resident can rely, divert, and redirect his or her inappropriate energies into productive, appropriate and acceptable behavior. For example, we could let them help us clean, or have the staff engage the resident in some type of recreation or work activity or redirect to a quite area away from whatever or whoever is causing episodes of inappropriate behavior. This is why a good and comprehensive medical and social history is of tremendous importance. It can be extremely helpful in defining not only the physical needs of a resident but also their likes and dislikes as well as those situations, experiences, and things, which are upsetting to them.

ANGER

Anger as a response to an emotional need is also common among the elderly residents. Anger usually follows frustration. Anger can be vented by the resident on either a verbal or physical basis, or both, toward us or something outside their comfort zone. It can exist in varying degrees from a sullen, withdrawn silence to proportions, which may result in aggression. Of the emotional responses of fear, anger, grief, hate and love, anger is probably the most dangerous with which the caregiver has to be concerned since there is less control present when a resident reacts angrily to a felt need. For example, a resident may shout, cry, threaten, or be destructive. As long as no harm is done to him or herself, another person, or to things in his or her environment, it is sometimes helpful to allow such expressions of anger. For, in this manner, he or she can "blow off steam". When the outburst is over, the resident can often be dealt with in a more effective manner than if interfered with during their outburst or inappropriate behavior. When a resident exhibits redundant behavior such as walking up and down his or her living area or talking loudly making inappropriate accusations toward specific persons such episodes of behavior can best be handled by redirection to a secluded area until he or she calms down. If we counterattack such behavior, it will usually continue and grow in intensity.

Anger is frequently associated with and directed towards oneself. If such is the case with a resident, his or her internalized anger may be accompanied by feelings of a dislike towards themselves. Residents who react in this manner are sometimes self-abusive, and as a result, pull their hair out, hit, slap, bite, scratch themselves or exhibit other self-abusive behavior. This type of resident requires constant attention and needs to be kept busy performing tasks, which they enjoy. We, whether directed inward or outward, should redirect anger. Then, too, if a punching bag is available, this exercise, is a good remedy for residents who have the stamina to participate in such an activity; so is bowling, or some passive work duties can be prescribed until the initial "heat" of anger has been spent. However, we should always attempt to determine the reason or object of a resident's anger, and share all information with medical or professional staff. One further observation regarding anger is that a resident's anger is seldom directed towards the caregiver personally. Often, it will appear this way because the resident may express verbal and even physical abuse toward another person, displacing their anger toward objects or things in their living environment.

GRIEF

Grief can best be defined as mental anguish, pain, sorrow, or distress. It is a baffling problem to residents and those who care for them because it is usually a deep-seated and subtle kind of reaction. The depression, which accompanies grief, is most frequently the result of the loss of a loved one by rejection, desertion, or death, although any failure or loss can produce depression. However, grief is a normal reaction to the loss of a friend, or loved one but it does not equal depression. The individual who is depressed often develops guilt, self-blame, and feels unrealistic responsibilities for the loss. Grief, on the other hand, results in the grief stricken individual wishing that they had done something different, but do not necessarily or persistently blame themselves. Until a substitute is defined and offered as a means of replacing a resident's loss or failure, the resident will suffer very real physical pains, and may develop suicidal tendencies. The resident who has lost someone they love very much is often slow to accept any kind of substitute, because they are plagued by memories of happier times and events, which bring forth new feelings of loneliness and despair. It is of the utmost importance that the resident who is experiencing grief be made aware of things outside themselves. In addition, if they are a religious person, who participates in church activities or has a close and frequent contact with parishioners is extremely helpful.

However, it is important to remember as a caregiver, that thoughts of self-destruction may be uppermost in the mind of the resident who is experiencing grief. The resident should be carefully observed at all times, without them being aware of it. We should encourage them to be an active participant in small group activities as much as possible. The sincere friendship and or bonding between the grieving resident and caregiver can provide them with enough stimuli to help the resident become aware of other people, objects and things in their environment. We should realize that time is an essential element in working with a grief stricken resident.

DEPRESSION

We as caregivers should be sensitive to our resident who has frequent episodes of depression. When a resident seems to always feel sad, unhappy, fatigued, listless, with feelings of hopelessness, or uninterested in life and what it has to offer we should suspect depression. There are other behaviors we should look for such as avoiding activities, loss of appetite, sleep, and complaints of such physical symptoms as weakness, fatigue, unexplained aches and pains, feeling useless and worthless, of being a burden, no longer loved or appreciated by anyone and significant weight loss. Depression should be recognized and taken seriously by us. We should seek the help from a mental health professional as the resident may become mired in excess deep-seated fear and denial until the more serious symptoms subside. We should also stick with the treatment strategies and report progress or the lack of progress and any side effects of medication being prescribed to attending medical staff. Small therapeutic activities can also help in the resident's recovery as he or she can tolerate.

MOOD

We should also closely monitor mood swings, especially if the resident's mood swings are frequent. We should look for or be aware of our resident's lack of insight into their behavior and do not consider themselves to be ill. Their behavior often consists of them being cheerful, but irritable. Their irritability may occur at the slightest provocation. Their self-confidence is characterized by highs and lows and their actions may be impulsive. They have a decreased need for sleep; have grandiose ideas, flighty thoughts and ideas, poor impulse control and unrealistic goals. We should involve this type of resident in small group activities, and maintain a kind but firm relationship with him or her helping them to focus on realistic ideas and subject matter. Stick closely with the treatment strategies of the team and report any side effects of medication and inappropriate behavior to the professional staff.

LOVE AND HATE

Contrary to popular belief, love and hate can and does exist together. These are two of the strongest emotional responses of which human beings are capable. Love, in particular, is a dominant factor throughout life. In the normal course of events, we love our families, friends, husband, wife, or significant other. We are also capable of deep spiritual emotions, love of objects and things and, most important, self-love. Love of another person implies many things – tolerance, understanding, companionship, respect, loyalty, all of which spell giving. Many residents are not capable of giving and live a self-centered, narrow life, frequently missing the happiness contained in sharing themselves, things and possessions with someone else.

This is called narcissism where the resident loves him or herself and is incapable of loving someone else considering their own body as their love object. As a caregiver, it is important for us to know this and refrain from taking such behavior personally. We should also be aware that he or she usually represents someone in the resident's past toward whom the resident has felt either love, hate or both. Therefore, if we have this knowledge we should not be offended if a resident dislikes us. Likewise, one must be careful that the resident who likes us does not become overly dependent on or attached to us. It is important to maintain a stable and consistent attitude toward all residents, since the resident is seeking a way to improve or at least maintain their present state of health. It is our responsibility to offer the resident a realistic plan of care to follow. A resident does not become overly attached or dependent without encouragement. We should never allow ourselves to become overly involved with our resident through any kind of strong emotional ties. In doing so, we only create more problems for a resident who is already struggling with chronic physical, mental and emotional problems to the point that he or she cannot function appropriately and independently within a community setting. Often, we do not recognize such over-attachments, which are a mistake since we should always attempt to divide our time evenly with the residents and to seek advice from others who are aware of this emotional response.

Hate, like grief, presents a challenge for us because it is a subtle reaction. Hate is usually well controlled and masked by all kinds of inappropriate behavior. Hate, or hostility, is expressed in many different ways – rejection, withdrawal, sarcasm, being overly kind and helpful, or flattery, and in the manipulation of pitting other residents and even caregivers against one another. Hate, being a nonproductive factor, must like anger be redirected. It may gradually wear itself out and be replaced by positive feelings and day-to-day activities which ultimately work for the common good. This is especially true if we never reward unacceptable or "bad" behavior.

It is tempting, however, for us in our interaction with residents and their emotional responses, to include happiness and satisfaction. However, these emotions do not represent needs. We are usually so concerned with the multiple, and at times, complex problems facing us that we rejoice in the sharing of any positive responses on the part of a resident. Emotions such as happiness and satisfaction often lull us into becoming part of the problem rather than the solution.

HELPFUL TIPS IN DEVELOPING POSITIVE ATTITUDES

A caregiver's attitude is vital to bonding and caring for a resident. Attitudes and responses to a resident's attitudes change constantly minute-by-minute, hour-by-hour and day-by-day. If we are prepared to meet the basic, dominant attitudes of the resident, we will also be able to meet the varying degrees of the resident's dominant attitudes. With so many complex issues, which demand our attention, we must react to them with patience, tact, interest and responsibility.

In many therapeutic situations, the theory of the importance of personal attitudes and their effect on residents has been developed to the point of prescribing attitudes. It is known as "attitude therapy". In relation to particular residents, the physician actually prescribes an attitude such as kindness, kind firmness, joviality, sympathy, which is to be done consistently--whatever the particular situation demands. The caregivers are expected to administer such attitudes much as they would administer any other specific mode of treatment.

CHAPTER THREE

DEVELOPING CAREGIVING SKILLS

Caregiving is a diverse activity, which takes many forms. For example, a resident may receive care individually, as a couple, or with the family in which the dynamics between family members will be the focus of service. The capacity and setting in which we as caregivers work also varies. Our services may range from a few hours a week doing voluntary work with an agency or organization to caring for a spouse or family member full time. In addition, we may work as a paid employee in a hospital, nursing home, institutional setting or work privately in a professional practice. In addition, we may provide services in areas of activities of daily living of a resident such as toileting, bathing, grooming, dressing, and dining, where there has been skill loss. We may also work with individuals who are experiencing mental, emotional and spiritual problems including dementia or with someone with a severe psychological condition. Furthermore, some of us may focus on medical conditions like cancer or other physical illnesses, disabilities, social problems such as alcohol, drug abuse, or a combination of such complex situations, which inhibit independent functioning on the part of the individual for whom we are caring. In addition, there is also end of life issues, the terminally ill, death, dying, grief and depression which further challenges our caregiving skills. Finally, adding to the complexity to our jobs is that we have to work with some basic knowledge of varying approaches in caring for individuals, which include behavioral, analytical, humanistic, social and spiritual perspectives.

Given that, there has been a proliferation of caregiving activity in the past forty years or so in our society; it seems likely that caregiving is fulfilling a need, which was, in the past, met by other means. Currently people who reside in the community, home care is fast becoming the preferred method of caring for the elderly with trained caregivers being available to provide care in the home rather than in long-term care facilities. Although there will always be a need for skilled care for the chronically ill, more and more emphasis is being placed on home care. Therefore, we caregivers will need to expand and sharpen our caregiving skills focusing on adding to our knowledge base the art of listening and responding skills, which will give us more choices about providing holistic care to the elderly who choose home care. It is also vital for those of us who work as caregivers to be aware of our limitations recognizing when we are out of our area of expertise. We should know when it is time to refer a person who needs help to deal with a specific medical or behavioral problem, to someone with appropriate training and experience for consultation and recommendations. The objective is not, after all, to overload ourselves with responsibilities for which we are not qualified, but rather to lighten our load by interacting and improving our relationships with professional personnel and support groups around us.

AWARENESS

As caregivers, sharpening our awareness is extremely important and we can do so by speaking, hearing, seeing, feeling and thinking. These areas of communication are all ways in which we respond and give attention to each other. During times of an emergency, we often have a heightened response to another who is in need or experiencing a crisis; at this point and time both head and heart goes into an operative mode.

In our concern for the elderly with dementia or Alzheimer's disease, we examine the most effective way to help them find relief from their predicament of memory and skill loss in activities of daily living. In doing so, we become highly focused. At other times, especially when strong emotions are involved, we are often at a loss about how we can be of any help to the elderly person. By identifying and developing simple strategies, we can enhance our ability to be more fully engaged for another person when they are experiencing difficulties in their lives trying to cope with the ravages of old age, dementia or Alzheimer's disease.

The basic skills that we use as a caregiver involve listening, observing, attending, and responding to a resident's needs. Active listening requires full attention, and alertness to every piece of behavior exhibited, and to what is both implicitly and openly said, thereby helping the resident to clarify confused feelings and thoughts. The ground rules, which help us respond effectively, include reflecting, paraphrasing and summarizing, appropriate questioning and empathy. Responding on an empathic level involves responding to content—to what the resident is verbally conveying—and to feelings tentatively reflecting back on our understanding of the feelings the resident is expressing.

USE OF QUESTIONS

Asking questions when communicating with a resident may seem the most natural thing to do during our interactions, but questioning can be overdone as well as being inappropriate. Questions can be intrusive, too forceful and threating. Many times, we ask questions to satisfy our own curiosity, none of which is beneficial in helping the resident; yet questions, when used tactfully and tentatively, are necessary for the exploration and clarification of facts and feelings of the resident for whom we are caring.

Questions by us who work as caregivers should be used sparingly because residents are generally encouraged to work on tasks to improve or maintain skill loss at their own pace. While receiving personal care, residents find many of the tasks on which they are working difficult. Many times painful material inevitably surfaces and insensitive questioning from us who serve as caregivers is destructive in bonding and building trust. One of the tenets of care provided by us is the belief that individuals can self-heal, that they possess an innate ability to recognize what they need and given the right set of circumstances and care can re-orientate themselves to what is meaningful to them in their lives. In other words, most of us resent other people telling us what to do, nor do we want others delving into our personal affairs. However, we do appreciate someone being with us in times, which are problematic, and listening attentively with sensitivity while we attempt to deal with our physical, mental, spiritual and emotional difficulties.

CLOSED QUESTIONS

When we as caregivers ask a closed question, it is usually met with a closed response—that is, a response that does not allow for any further discussion or exploration. Closed questions are useful for informational gathering when we need to know specific facts. For example, during an intake session with a new resident, when we note personal, medical, social and work details, etc.; the answer to a closed question is often "yes, no, or I don't know." The closed question begins: "Do you, can't you, have you, is it, would you say, could it, don't you think", and so on. The problem with questioning which invites a "yes" or "no" type of reply is that it can leave us both as the caregiver and the resident facing a blank wall and lead to more questioning. While we are bombarding someone with questions, their feelings are subdued. In contrast, open questions allow further exploration of meanings, thoughts, and feelings, as well as encouraging the resident to impart additional material.

It is a good idea when using questions to ask ourselves what the purpose is, and if it is assisting or hindering us in the helping process. We may be gathering information when it would be more appropriate to wait, giving the resident time to get in touch with his or her feelings associated with what he or she is telling us. The excessive use of questioning by an inexperienced caregiver can be a ploy adopted to distance ourselves from the resident. For example, this occurs when we are uncomfortable with our own feelings concerning what the resident is expressing or with silences during our interaction. A golden rule, when communicating with a resident, is to use our ears and eyes more than our mouth!

WHY? WHY NOT?

"Why" is best used sparingly by the caregiver. Think of a question like: "Why did you do that"? Moreover, how loaded it is. The word 'why" implies that the answer is accessible. It may involve validation or denial of the resident's actions, which can result in a defensive response. "Why" can often sound accusatory. It may seem as expressing displeasure or disapproval and it may have associations with past feelings of getting "things wrong". "Why" is also difficult to answer in relation to our feelings. It can take the resident into a "thinking" mode as part of an intellectual rationalization exercise, which avoids the world of emotions. Not surprisingly a question like "Why do you feel this way"? or "Why do you think that"? is more than likely than not to be met with a shrug and "I don't know", which may result in the resident losing track of what they are thinking and feeling.

WHAT WE NEED TO KNOW

The society in which we reside is changing and will most likely continue to do so. It is complex, demanding, and dysfunctional. The elderly is living longer and requiring more services, which are challenging. Such circumstances can result in the caregiver experiencing undue stress and frustration, which often causes physical and mental difficulties. Further complicating our role as a caregiver is that many of us no longer live in supportive communities bound together by social values, religious faith and similar beliefs; we live in fragmented societies alienated, at times, from our surroundings and each other. Our horizons and the world in which we live have expanded; the towns and cities where we live and work, both large and small, are impersonal. Therefore, the meaning and role of caregiving is ever evolving to meet the challenges of modern social pressures, needs and demands, which we often attempt to deal with at a cost to our inner world.

The role of caregiving may best be defined by its aims and values. Aims include providing an environment that enables the resident to work towards living in a more resourceful and personally fulfilling way. Integrity, respect and impartiality are basic values, which should be demonstrated throughout the caregiving process.

Caregiving in our society is increasingly multifaceted and always supportive. As society progresses, caregiving, it seems, will continue to be very much a part of our lives, no longer regarded as a luxury or indulgence. Caregiving is seen for the most part as a sensible move towards self-care during one's life's journey. The majority of us have an open mind about the service provided by a caregiver, taking the view that anything that is nurturing, supportive, and self-enlightening is needed, useful and helpful in today's busy and dysfunctional world.

OPEN QUESTIONS

As caregivers, we should communicate with the resident utilizing the open question method. Open questions are valuable because they enable both the caregiver and resident alike to express their thoughts, feelings, and personal meanings. They invite the other person to talk, to communicate and self-explore. They allow time to explore situations, open questions begin with "how, when, where, what", and "in what way". The answers given by the resident allows the caregiver to gain a clearer understanding of the resident's difficulties and put them in a position to assist the resident to be more specific.

An example of an open question is as follows: "I'm not clear what you mean when you tell me that your stomach hurts. Could you give me an example"? Clarifying non-direct questions can be useful to the caregiver in the care that they provide. For example, "Can you explain to me exactly where you hurt"? encouraging elaboration of points on the part of the resident. This type of questioning also requires the resident to be reflective. Open questions, however, have no "right or wrong answers".

MULTIPLE QUESTIONS

As a caregiver, we should not ask too many questions—be sparing, do not be too intrusive. It is important for us as caregivers to respect the resident's right to privacy. Some issues may be too sensitive, delicate, and too intimate to pursue too quickly. We should allow time for bonding and trust to develop. The resident, especially during the early periods of care when it is crucial to establish trust, may feel interrogated rather than being supported by the caregiver. This will be non-productive and impede the building of rapport. The frequent use of questions too soon does not allow time for the exploration of thoughts and feelings when they arise; personal care can then be experienced as confusing as the caregiver's interest appears to be initiated on a superficial level only. We as caregivers must be aware of using multiple questions, with one question superseding another in a string of inquires. This can be experienced as annoying and distracting as well as confusing and gives little indication of the caregiver's competence.

We should ask one question at a time and then listen with full attention given to the response.

When we engage the resident, we should use questions appropriately rather than bombarding the resident with one question after another. It helps to instill the habit of placing questioning in context with other skills during the caring process. Questions form a small part of skills use. Skills like paraphrasing, reflecting feelings and content along with other methods of attentive responding motivate the resident to talk openly and freely.

LEADING QUESTIONS

Leading questions imply answers that the caregiver would find acceptable. Leading, or biased questions can effectively stop the resident from expressing their thoughts and feelings for fear of being ridiculed. For example: "You're not thinking of leaving the nursing home, are you"? On the other hand, "You're not going to cry, are you"? These types of question consist of an instructive statement: "You wouldn't give up your room", followed by a question, "Would you"? The first part of the question tells the resident what to do, and then the second appears to give an opinion. This is not empathic sensitive questioning, it is judgmental, restrictive, and will do little to enhance the relationship.

QUESTIONS TO ASK OURSELVES AS CAREGIVERS

- Am I trying to clear up a point? (Clarifying).
- Am I gathering information?
- Does my question help the resident to explore his or her situation?

- Does my question have any therapeutic value?
- Am I avoiding anything by asking a question?
- Am I trying to put the resident at ease?
- Do I perceive questioning as making the resident or me uncomfortable?

Asking too many questions can be an attempt to force change or to control the direction of care; both can cause the resident to deflect from issues rather than going into them. We should let the resident move at his or her own pace; the point after all is to lessen as much anxiety as we can, not to add more to it. There is a role for challenging a resident when we feel they will benefit from it, however, a caregiver should always be well advised to challenge the resident cautiously, respecting the resident's right to address certain issues regarding their care in their own time.

SOME GENERAL RULES FOR ASKING QUESTIONS DURING THE CAREGIVING PROCESS

- Use open questions when possible.
- Avoid using closed questions, which invite a yes or no answer.
- Use closed questions when seeking specific information.
- Use indirect questions as a softer approach.
- Use questions sparingly.
- Be aware that some form of questioning may suggest disapproval or criticism.
- Use one appropriate question at a time.
- Check the purpose of your question before proceeding.
- Be aware of your tone of voice, the speed of your questions, how it is delivered and the message it may convey.

TO EVALUATE THE PURPOSE OF YOUR QUESTION

- To clarify—to assist the resident be more concrete and specify with their responses.
- To help the resident identify problems and the factors which have created them?
- To gain useful information.
- To help us as caregivers to gain and maintain a clear understanding of the resident's situation.
- To help the resident get in touch with his or her emotions.
- To get a reality check—i.e. did I get that right? Does it have a specific meaning? I wonder what it means.
- To explore underlying thoughts, feelings, meanings.
- To enable or encourage further insight into what has been said, cue behavior, or done, leading to unexplored material regarding his or her care, i.e. psychosocial information such as marriage, spouse, children, relatives, life's work, etc.

EXAMPLES OF OPEN/CLOSED QUESTIONS

1. (a) Closed question: Were you upset when that happened?
   (b) Open question: How did you feel when that happened?
2. (a) Closed question: Could you quit drinking if you really wanted to?
   (b) Open question: What kind of problems do you think you might encounter if you tried to stop drinking?
3. (a) Closed question: Do you still miss your husband?
   (b) Open question: Tell me how you feel about your husband?

4. (a) Closed question: Could it be that you start arguments with your children?

(b) Open question: What happens when you and your children argue?

5. (a) Closed question: Were you sad when your husband died?

(b) Open question: How did you feel when your husband died?

Number four (4) is an example of how a closed question can also be challenging. Open questions focus on feelings as well as content.

Unlike the (a) questions, the (b) questions address associated feelings in that they invite the resident to talk about feelings such as fear, hurt, and dependency. Number two (a) could be experienced as a challenge such as a judgmental remark relating to strength or weakness of character. In contrast, Number 2 (b) is a more empathic form of questioning acknowledging the possible difficulty of the task.

Notice the language that we use when questioning a resident. The word "quit" in Number 2 (a) may be appropriate to use, depending on the language the resident uses, but it could add to the sense of being challenged. The words, if one wanted to, could also be loaded with implications if taken out of context with what the resident has been saying. It could seem that we are suggesting that they do not really want to give up and be received as a criticism.

THE USE OF EMPATHY

Empathy can be described, and has been by many of us who work as caregivers, as entering into another person's frame of reference. Others describe empathy as the caregiver having the ability to experience life's journey as the other person does by temporarily entering into the resident's world of thoughts, meanings and feelings. In reality, empathy is an expression of the regard and respect the caregiver holds for the resident. We should hold in high esteem the resident's frame of reference to the human aspects of his or her life such as values, thoughts, meanings, feelings, cultural influences, experiences and beliefs may be quite different from our own. We should never lose ourselves in the resident's belief system. It is important that we as caregivers retain our own sense of self. We would be of little use if we began sobbing uncontrollably when a resident was struggling to express his or her grief. This is a caricature of a situation, but serves to make a point. The resident needs to feel "held" as well as understood. True empathic responding does both. To be held therapeutically means to feel that we are capable of accepting and supporting a resident through anything that he or she is trying to cope. We as caregivers convey to the resident that we are unjudgmental, unskockable and strong enough not to have to be protected from what we may envision as being unacceptable behavior. It can be a healthy and therapeutic relief to admit all and let go of what we think as being inappropriate thoughts, feelings and condition and meet such behaviors with an accepting, empathic response.

Empathic responding circumnavigates all the other skills. Our ability to empathize with the resident is enhanced by an ever-alert attentiveness to facial expressions, body language, gestures, not only to what is being said or openly conveyed but also to the underlying implications. Intuition, "gut" or "hunches" have a part to play in empathic responding.

EMPATHY VERSUS SYMPATHY

Empathy is often confused with sympathy. When we feel sympathy for our residents, we view them with pity. "Poor John. He can't cope with the death of his wife." Pity is often linked with victim-hood. While pity makes a victim of the one, who is suffering, empathy empowers them. It says: "I have a sense of your inner world—you do not stand alone, we will make this journey together." The other person becomes an important subject rather than an object whose problems are far removed from us. We can tell we are objectifying someone when in our minds we put him or her into a slot--a sociological category or stereotype like "the abandoned husband", or "the single spouse." These classifications stifle empathic understanding, which relates to each individual and views their experience as being unique.

AWARENESS OF BODY LANGUAGE

As caregivers, we must be aware that our inner emotional state is communicated through our bodies. We give each other messages through our body movements, the intonation of our voice, facial expressions, posture, gestures and our eye contact all send messages to the resident. Some of these movements may be slight or fleeting but in the heightened atmosphere of one-to-one care, they are more often than not registered when we care for others. We need to be aware of two sets of body language, 1) our own and 2) that of the resident for whom we are caring. As a caregiver, our body needs to demonstrate behavior that is important. One is "adverse stimulus." This occurs when we display an attitude, which is "putting off" to the resident. We may display signs of non-attention. For example, looking bored, yawning, fidgeting or showing a lack of interest, all conveys to the resident our lack of concern regarding their needs. Another example of advice stimulus is "punitive attention." This occurs when we look stern, tight-lipped, raising our eyebrows or staring fixedly at the resident. It is not difficult to appreciate how this type of behavior by us as caregivers acts as a deterrent to accessing any material, of which the resident senses that we as a caregiver may disapprove.

Other mannerisms like picking at or cleaning our fingernails, shrugging or sniffing can be distracting to the resident. This all seems so obvious and we may think we avoid all of such behavior, but it can be a revelation to monitor ourselves when caring for the resident.

POSTURE

Our posture reveals the degree of interest we have for the resident. When we interact with the resident, keeping a safe distance or ignoring a task, which should be performed, we display an attitude of lack of interest. Similarly, when we cross our arms and legs, we convey a message that we are less open to the resident's input or complaints. We are in some way protecting ourselves from bonding or shutting out the resident. In contrast, a relaxed and attentive posture conveys to the resident that we are comfortable with ourselves and with the resident or members of their family. Although it would be unnatural, it is with everything in life, there are always exceptions to these rules and at times, what seems to be a mistake often proves to be useful. It is good to learn these skills and also retain as much of ourselves as possible so that we respond in both a spontaneous and appropriate manner. An example is that if we find ourselves crossing of arms or legs during our interaction with our resident, rather than thinking "Oh no, I shouldn't be doing this," it is more useful to observe yourself and make a mental note, "I have my arms and legs crossed, I wonder why? Perhaps I am uncomfortable with what is being expressed, or it may be that in some way I am reflecting what my resident is feeling."

A caregiver who is caring for his or her resident often finds themselves yawning at times throughout his or her interaction with the resident, in the spirit of being honest might say to the resident something to the effect. "I'm yawning again and I can see that you feel that I am neglecting you. I do feel tired. I've had a rough week." It is important for the caregiver in situations like this to be "real", showing and making a genuine effort to be direct and honest about his or her inappropriate behavior towards the resident.

TONE OF VOICE

The tone of our voice serves as an indicator of our thoughts, feelings and attitudes. If we speak too quietly or hesitantly, the resident may find it difficult to have confidence in us as a caregiver or of our skills. It would be counterproductive to be too forceful in the way we interact with the resident. If, as caregivers, we talk clearly at a steady level rather than sounding rushed or excited and without mumbling or stumbling over our words, then we are probably getting it right. Sometimes it is appropriate to mirror the tone of the resident's voice to help them hear the emotion conveyed.

Although humor can be useful at times, when used sparingly, it is not a good idea to adopt a manner of joking with our residents. It can inhibit their expression of deeper underlying feelings or inhibit their ability to express their needs. It is neither the caregivers nor the resident's obligation to entertain or cheer up the other. In fact, this approach would totally defeat the effectiveness and benefits of the caregiving process.

WORDS AND BODY LANGUAGE

Words can be either congruent or incongruent with what our body is demonstrating both on the part of the caregiver and on the part of resident alike. For example, we may say "I understand" while looking perplexed, or say, "no, that doesn't surprise me in the least" having raised our eyebrows and crossed our arms and legs. What the body is doing is an indicator of deeper, sometimes unconscious feelings. A common display of incongruence is when a resident says that they are angry while smiling, or that they are deeply sad with no emotion whatsoever. This tells us that the resident is not comfortable in expressing their true emotions. What the resident and caregiver hear is reinforced or contradicted by what they see demonstrated by the body language of the other.

THE RESIDENT'S BODY LANGUAGE

While we as caregivers need to be aware of our own body language, it is also important that we work, during our caregiving duties, to decode, understand, and interpret the body language of our residents. What does their body language tell us? Body and facial expression can inform us a great deal about their hidden feelings. For example:

He or she is angry. His or her mouth is tensed. His or her eyes are narrowed and leaning back in chair or if in bed turns his or her head away from the caregiver avoiding eye contact.

He or she is very upset and near tears. He or she has placed his or her hand up to forehead and mouth is twitching. He or she, if sitting, leans slightly forward in chair with head down.

He or she is eager to be understood. He or she leans forward toward the caregiver with feet placed firmly on the floor; he or she gestures freely with hands, talking intently with eyes fixed on the caregiver.

REFLECTING SKILLS OF THE RESIDENT

Paraphrasing, summarizing and mirroring are all ways of reflecting back the resident's thoughts and feelings. They are all important methods of reiterating a resident's expression in order that:

- The resident can hear again, what they are saying.
- The resident can get a sense of him or herself, i.e., how they are expressing themselves, as if a mirror was being held up before them.
- The caregiver is able to check and crosscheck what they are receiving and how they are understanding and interrupting— meanings, thoughts and feelings are correct.
- There is clarification of certain points on the part of the caregiver without asking questions, which are intrusive.
- The interpretation of the material can be more meaningful and manageable for both the caregiver and resident alike.
- The material can insure on-going communication between the caregiver and resident making the job of caregiving more meaningful for both of them.
- The lines of communication and interaction can be joined together making their relationship a more coherent whole.

PARAPHRASING

Paraphrasing is reflecting back on the content and feelings of what the resident is saying by drawing out the salient parts of what is said and observed during the caregiving process. The content is usually repeated in the caregivers own words, which gives a slightly different perspective on the material discussed with the resident. Paraphrasing is best used at natural intervals or when it seems appropriate to reiterate what is being conveyed. It lets the resident know what you are following what he/she says and that you are attentive to their personal details and understanding of their feelings and their meanings. It is not the case that because the resident has spoken then the caregiver is immediately required to paraphrase the details; it is instead a matter of sensitively gauging when it is appropriate to use the skill of paraphrasing.

As individuals, caregivers will paraphrase differently, as with all the skills there is no absolute set formula. Caregivers should develop a style with which they are comfortable. Some caregivers talk more than others do, while some may place emphasis on emphasizing one or more topics during the paraphrasing process than others. It depends on the maturity, and skills of the caregiver.

EXAMPLES OF PARAPHRASING

1. (a) The resident's comment.
When I was a young girl, I used to wish my father would leave. At the time I visualized that, he was dead—because he was angry and took out his hostility on me. When he did die, a few years later, I had mixed   feelings of love and hate as well as both relief and sadness. However, the relief I felt because he was gone and could

no longer abuse me made me feel guilty. Now that I am older I still feel guilty and ashamed when I think about some of the thoughts I had about him and the things I said and did to him while he was alive.

(b) The caregiver's response.

For a long time now, most of your life you have felt guilty about your negative feelings and actions towards your father when he was alive. He could be and perhaps was extremely and unreasonably harsh with you at times and when he died, you must have felt both a sense of freedom as well as sadness. Feeling words are guilty, negative, harsh, freedom, sadness.

2. (a) The resident's comment.

My grandson lived with his father, (my daughter is deceased) in another town. When he used to visit, I became irritated at times because he was always demanding, wanting things I could not afford and asking questions in great detail about my personal life. He usually inquired about how much money his grandfather and I had in our possession, and he expected me to be a constant source of entertainment during his infrequent visits.

(b) The caregiver's response.

When your grandson comes to visit you, you perhaps feel overwhelmed by his need for your love, affection, and attention. You may feel irritated by his inquiries and invasion into your personal life and you wish he could be less self-centered and more self-sufficient while he visits with you. Feeling words are: overwhelmed, love, affection, attention, irritated and personal life.

3. (a) The resident's comment.

I broke up with my husband. I divorced him. It was my fault because I felt claustrophobic having to spend most of time at home as a housewife. I was restless and felt my husband was controlling me. After my divorce, I found living on my own a difficult experience.

(b) The caregiver's response.

You left a relationship because you felt stifled by it and unable to express yourself while you were in the relationship, but you found it hard living alone and sometimes missed your ex-spouse. Feeling words: stifled, express yourself, hard living alone and missed.

4. (a) The resident's comment.

When it gets dark, I feel afraid, lonely with a sense of emptiness. I have a life void of meaningful issues and do not know how to fill it.

Sometimes I wind up drinking alcoholic drinks to cope with my feelings, which in a sense keeps me occupied, and although I know I have a drinking problem I do not feel I have the motivation to fill the void with something more meaningful or creatively.

(b) The caregiver's response.

You drink in the evening because you feel emptiness inside. You are low in self-esteem and feel unable to tackle the problem in a self-nurturing manner. Feeling words: emptiness inside, low, unable, tackle, self-nurturing.

To recap, paraphrasing consists of the following:

- Gives the resident an opportunity to hear what they are saying, in a slightly different context, which can lead to a new insight.
- Is a way of reflecting the content and feelings of what the resident is saying.
- Entails content and feelings being reflected back in the caregiver's own words.
- Demonstrates the caregivers caring attitude and attentiveness.

- Gives the resident an opportunity to clarify anything the caregiver does not understand and the caregiver an opportunity to check and crosscheck to see if they are getting it right.
- It is a method of maintaining contact with the resident to strengthen bonding insuring a positive relationship.

In summary, these examples of responses reflect back, in the caregiver's own language, the content of what the resident has related and also the resident's feelings.

MIRRORING

Mirroring, which bears a resemblance to parroting, has to be used with sensitivity to be well received by and useful to the resident. The caregiver mirrors, for example, by repeating a line the resident has said or mirroring an expression. However, mirroring an expression is not straight mimicking and it should be done in a subtle manner. For example, the resident might say; "I am enjoying my new room – it's big and a challenge but I like challenges most of the time", with a grimace at the end of the statement. You may have noticed that he has mixed feelings about his new room and may be wondering if he has made the right decision in choosing it or doubting if he is up to getting used to it. To check this out, you may choose to subtly mirror the grimace and notice his words. "Most of the time" ----- this could be useful to him, leading into examining what it is he is not happy with, perhaps a challenge in his life that he has not yet mentioned.

SUMMARIZING

Summarizing is similar in many ways to paraphrasing. However, it requires the joining together of larger pieces of information gained from the resident. This occurs after the resident has communicated with the caregiver for a lengthy period of time. While paraphrasing is relevant to one piece of information regardless of the length, or size summarizing links together a few or many statements made by the resident. It is a way for the caregiver to maintain contact with the resident, showing that he/she as caregivers are following what they are saying and that they have an understanding of their needs including their underlying feelings. Another purpose of summarizing is that it brings together different trends of what has been expressed, providing an overview which enables the resident to make connections.

There may be an overall theme, which can be brought together by summarizing. For example, a resident may spend a lot of time during the caregiving process saying how low he or she feels about different relationships they have experienced with others. And although the story differs each time it is told, a unifying theme emerges. Their father was cold, distance, critical and indifferent of them—no matter how much they tried to please him, his wife tolerated him, was unresponsive, showing little affection and those he considered his friends had little time for him. The resident felt such relationships contributed to their own low self-esteem and present illness.

We as a caregiver, can connect these themes together by giving a summary of the different things that have been said by the resident. Also, then by adding an interpretative summary like: "I think what you are saying is that, although you tried your best to get close to those who mattered to you, you feel that they did not respond to you in the way that you would have liked." An underlying theme may be repeated throughout the caregiving process or even after the story has been told repeatedly. We as a caregiver can continue to summarize the information as it can sharpen the resident's perception as to what lies behind the repetitive thoughts, feelings and behavior. It can also be vital when shared with other members of the team involved in the resident's care. For example, during his or her interaction with the resident, the caregiver gets to know the resident best and can share information that can be extremely useful in providing care.

The point of both paraphrasing and summarizing is to assist the resident in further exploration of troubling issues, to help the resident reach new insights into their illness. It is especially important when summarizing a lot of accumulated information to conclude with an inquiry about the accuracy or our understanding of the information. We can check this out by saying to the resident, "Is that how you feel?" or "Does that sum it up?" or simply "Am I getting what you are saying right?" Otherwise, those in the caregiving role may go off on an agenda of their own. The caregiver should use their own language to reflect back and try not to use standard phrases as these can sound stiff and unmeaningful and may be interpreted by the resident as being insincere. The idea is to learn skills, and not set formulas. When the caregiver becomes familiar with such skills, they can trust themselves to use their positive qualities to ascertain what is needed in the resident's overall care.

To Recap the Uses of Summarizing:
- It can be useful at intervals in the caregiving process to give a sense of connection between trends and/or themes of what the resident has been communicating to the caregiver.

- It gives the resident an overview of their situation, and life experiences, which may be affecting their illness.
- It is useful during the caregiving process, which highlight the resident's central concerns.

USING MINIMAL RESPONSES

Minimal responses are made to demonstrate the caregiver's attentiveness and understanding of what is said and to encourage the resident to continue. Minimal responses include the following:

- Mmm, Uh-huh.
- Nodding.
- Using one word such as "so", and, "then".
- Repeating one or a few key words the resident has used.
- Restating the exact words of the resident's statement apart from placing it in the second person, e.g. The resident says, "I feel so stupid", the caregiver says: "You feel so stupid". This is particularly useful when the comment is uttered as a throwaway line that may be covering a deeper hurt.
- Silence is another form of minimal response that allows the resident time to think, feel and find an appropriate expression or response.

WORDS

The resident often uses words to communicate how he or she feels about their age, illness and inner emotions. It is often extremely difficult for a resident to say, "I completely lost control, and I was destructive in my behavior, when I was in a rage". The word "rage" means a lot more than being "angry". The word "joy" is more revealing than "happy"; the word "morose" more specific than "sad" or "depressed". The word "devastated" more emotionally charged than "hurt", etc. Moreover, there are many more feeling words we can use to describe a resident's emotions.

However, a word of caution is due here because as caregivers we may have, at times, a different understanding of a particular word or phrase from that of the resident. Therefore, it is important to check and make sure that our understanding of a word corresponds with that of the residents and his or her concept of it's meaning. Residents whose culture values or background which is different from ours as caregivers may use a word in which we are unfamiliar. In paraphrasing and summarizing, we should use our own words to reflect back to them their understanding; the words which we use may put emphasis on feeling, offering the resident more insight. For example, a resident might say, "I am tired", and in paraphrasing, the caregiver might say, "you are exhausted". This may lead the resident to say, "Yes, I am exhausted", "I really don't think I can go on like this", leading to a cathartic release of emotion.

SILENCES

Managing silence means having the ability to recognize a constructive silence. It may take some time and patience for us to feel comfortable with periods of silence. Therefore, we should ask ourselves the following questions:

- How comfortable am I with being silent?
- How often do I spend time by myself in silence?
- Do I find silence to be productive?
- What associations do I have with silence?

Allowing silences gives the resident space to reflect. We may experience awkwardness at handling silence as a caregiver but as our threshold of a silence approach increases with experience, we will be able to discern between different types and be more comfortable implementing the silence approach. There are times when the resident is nervous, especially in the beginning, and a protracted silence may be experienced as excruciatingly uncomfortable. In this case, it would be advisable to acknowledge what we understand to be uncomfortable on their behalf and say something like "I imagine it is difficult for you to be here". This will serve two purposes. They are:

1. It breaks an uncomfortable silence.

2. It is likely to lead to disclosure of his or her feelings,

Residents can and do get lost in their own thoughts and feelings or at least feel overwhelmed by them, and a silence may then occur. A summary of what we as caregivers have understood can be useful at such a time. Sometimes a silence begins because the resident is hoping for something from the caregiver; this might be reassurance or confirmation that we as a caregiver has been listening, or has understood what has been said.

SHARPENING ONE'S SKILLS AS A CAREGIVER

- Learn to be patient. Listen carefully and attentively.
- Avoid being defensive or aggressive when interacting with the resident.
- Use one's abilities of observation—noticing the resident's body language, appearance, gestures, posture, eye contact and tone of voice.
- Avoid bombarding the resident with questions.
- Use questions to open up what the resident is trying to

convey and to expand one's understanding of his or her thoughts, feelings, and meanings.

- Paraphrase in one's own words to the resident as a means of checking and clarifying the content of what is being said and the feelings behind them.

- Use minimal responses such as "yes, ma'am", "yes sir", nodding, etc. to demonstrate one's attention, to show that the resident's comments are being followed and to encourage verbal communication and to encourage further exploration.

- Summarize after the resident has talked for a while in order to keep track and to join themes of what the resident has said. This helps us as a caregiver of checking and helping the resident see the overall picture.

- Use immediacy to address present issues in the relationship.

- Use challenging and confrontation with the resident cautiously and selectively. Examine one's motives before doing so. Do not use them to accuse, humiliate, or as act of revenge. The caregiver should instead examine their own agenda and challenge the behavior, not the resident because it should always be their aim to help the resident in a positive and constructive way.

- Use confrontation only when a resident exhibits inappropriate behavior.

An appropriate time to use confrontational skills is when the resident becomes rude or angry towards others or is repeatedly demonstrating destructive behavior. However, the caregiver must remember the aim of confrontation. It is intended to achieve a greater understanding of the resident's problem. However, one must at all times be aware of whose needs are being met by the confrontation. Does the caregiver, for example, need to express their own frustration, irritability or stress? If so, it may be more productive to use immediacy skills of addressing what is happening between the resident and caregiver. The two must be "real" themselves. Tell the resident about any personal feelings if they are in conflict with helping. For example, "I would like to help but I am frightened, angry or upset", but convey this information in a way that is not dismissive or rejecting of the resident.

CHAPTER FOUR

ETHICAL OBLIGATIONS

Throughout the course of our daily living, it is essential that we as human beings develop relationships with others, both individually and collectively. The few individuals in our society who prefer to live a secluded lifestyle are frequently classified in psychiatric texts as having a "schizoid personality disorder". We know that they have some emotional maladjustment, for human beings obviously need companionship. We must have contact with others from the human species in order to function adequately in our particular culture. It does not take us as a caregiver long to realize that a resident who is extremely sick retreats from contact with others. In some instances when the resident has been ill for a long period of time he or she will more than likely be completely unaware of their significant other's name, although they have lived together for years. Actually, the resident, in reality, may want to know and to be close to their spouse, significant other or neighbor. However, "running away" has always been his or her defense against being hurt for so long that they have forgotten such emotional human traits as warmth, love, forgiveness and other social skills.

Therefore, accepting the fact that people need to relate to and interact with others, we must also conclude that such relationships are going to be either good or bad, pleasant or unpleasant. One of the most important elements of success or failure of a relationship between two individuals is respect. Respect for the rights, beliefs and actions of another person pays him or her a hugh compliment. Respect for one's fellow man is fundamental to the successful and comforting care of a resident who is in our service. This important feeling is too often lost in a deluge of respect for ourselves. Satisfying our own needs and building our own security, unhappily at the cost of others, regresses to an old saying, "it is easier to criticize rather than to understand".

No illness is looked upon more critically with more fear and with less understanding than the elderly resident who is acutely sick and experiencing a behavioral problem or severe mental illness. When confronted with such a critical situation the caregiver should maintain a fundamental respect for the resident. We should seize on every opportunity to involve the family and community at large on just how much respect means to the resident. This is especially true when caring for the elderly with complex physical, mental and emotional issues. Such information, however, should be shared with both the professional and lay community alike in an honest, factual, straight forward and sincere manner.

PRIVACY

Gossip about a resident should never be done or tolerated. Bits and pieces of gossip about a resident, dropped here and there, can do harm to the resident and family. It is normal and is part of daily living to talk about things and events with others. Since people interact and work together and become interested in one another, to varying degrees, the caregiver should be aware that discussing an illness and care being provided a resident should be done in a cautious manner. It should always be done in a professional way to the resident's physician, and other professional personnel or family members. The major reason for this is often that malicious gossip or inappropriate information must not get back to the resident, family, or the public at large. In reality, any information regarding the resident and his or her care should never be revealed to anyone outside the family except as necessary among those who are actually working with the resident. Any illness is a deeply personal and revealing experience. Events leading up to an illness, such as behaviors associated with mental, emotional, dementia or Alzheimer's disease often involves not only intimate facts about the resident but also about those individuals closest to the resident, family, friends, or business associates. We, as caregivers, in his or her close contact with the resident, see and hear many intimate things, which the average and/or healthy person would never exhibit or admit. The innate respect for the resident should keep the caregiver from repeating such matters anywhere other than necessary about his or her job, except to a nurse, physician, or appropriate family member regarding the resident and the specific care being provided. A good example of this is when a caregiver was overheard to remark to a resident's daughter regarding her mother who was suffering from dementia, "Oh, she's a real problem. She attempts to masturbate every time I turn my head." The horrified daughter was not even sure of the meaning of the word and immediately and tearfully related the caregiver's comment to a group of her neighbors. When she found out the true meaning of masturbation, she remained in her house for days due to her embarrassment because she could not believe her mother would do such a thing. It was unnecessary and was certainly not helpful for the caregiver to have made such a remark. How indicative is it that the caregiver may be having difficulties with her own feelings about the resident's masturbating tendencies. There is no doubt that there are many times when actions or language, or both, will shock us as caregivers. However, judgment cannot be made about the resident since we cannot assume that what is wrong with us is equally so for the resident. A resident's behavior is always meaningful to them. To feel that a resident will offend others or will be punished is an undesirable effect resulting from a showing of the caregivers own feelings regarding behavior. In other words, it is acceptable to have such feelings. In fact, it is to be expected, but it is not acceptable to communicate them to the resident or to others. Moreover, it is unethical and illegal to talk out of school due to "privacy laws". Although it is inevitable that there will be "some talk" among professionals, the same rules should be applied. When a resident is being discussed, the caregiver should stop and think: "What am I saying? Is this something that would hurt or offend me if I were sick? Is this story any of my business?" Another example of damage resulting from gossip admitted by a caregiver to whom it actually happened is as follows: She and another caregiver were riding home together in a crowded bus. They were discussing an elderly man who had dementia to whom they had begun providing services a few days before. Using their full names, they laughed and joked about their extreme episodes of inappropriate behavior. Then one of the caregivers said to the other, "Their son is the president of the city school board." A newspaper reporter for the town's local paper was sitting behind them overheard their comments and summed their conversation up the following day in the newspaper: "The president of the school board parents are reported to be insane." Previously, a successful candidate for the position of president of the school board, the man lost the next election for the position he held and there was little doubt as to the reason for it.

Dementia and Alzheimer's disease and associated inappropriate behavior among the elderly are never a joke, nor should it be treated lightly. The caregiver knows, or should know, very well the heartbreak, the desolate loneliness, the hopeless anger that his or her resident feels remembering that this should make the caregiver respect confidentiality.

PROFESSIONAL PERSONNEL AND CONFIDENTALITY

Because so much attention is now being given to the elderly in the community, especially those with dementia, and Alzheimer's disease with associated behavior problems, gossip among professional personnel caregivers is inevitable. Technically speaking, the term gossip refers to a rumor or rumors without any factual basis.

It is perfectly natural for people to talk about one another, since a person is naturally curious about the interests and the background of friends and others. Such curiosity is healthful and best satisfied by questioning or feeling out the involved person. He or she is the one who knows the true facts, and it is likely that, in a sincere friendship, he or she would be willing to reveal any desired information. Unfortunately, many individuals have not always learned to "talk honestly" with one another. Therefore, a person often feels it necessary to make up groundless stories of misinformation about others in order to cover up for their lack of knowledge and/or abilities. The following story is true, taken from a publication on the subject of gossip. The material demonstrates how damaging thoughtless remarks can be. As the story goes, a resident walked to the nursing station in a nursing home to inquire about his clothing. As he approached the station, he heard one of the caregiver's comment, "Where was Dr. Doe last night? We tried to find him when John became upset during which time he exhibited aggressive and inappropriate behavior." The caregiver answered: "Oh! He was probably at some club or favorite watering hole getting drunk, as usual! He's in all reality, sicker than his patients!" As a result, the resident became extremely upset after hearing these comments, and refused any further treatment from the physician. The resident was, as a result of such gossip, suspicious of all other personnel thereafter, and it took a long time for the resident to regain his trust in his caregivers.

This is an example of how malicious gossip can be, and how quickly and easily a simple bit of misinformation can grow and interfere with the caring process between the resident and his or her caregiver. Another illustration is as follows: A caregiver had become involved in some trouble with the police in his hometown. They asked him to drive to court with them and he left the resident in the care of his family while he accompanied the officers to the police station and later to court. Within a very short time, the incident was all over the community that the caregiver had to be dragged to the police vehicle, aggressively resisting arrest, by four or five officers. Actually, the caregiver had walked peacefully and uneventful to the police station accompanied by one detective in plain clothes.

Gossip is sometimes used as a method of "getting even". This is particularly true when there is a lot of negative feelings among personnel providing various kinds of care and needs for a resident, i.e. "guarding one's turf." The person whose job it is to direct or share sensitive information is often the victim of considerable negative comments and gossip. Most often, such stories, negative comments, or just plain unfounded gossip are circulated merely to lower the individuals personal and professional abilities in the eyes of others—to discredit them.

Therefore, the caregiver who would not want his or her name banished about in a mesh of untruths and malicious gossip should avoid at all costs in becoming an active participant is such unprofessional and unethical activities. The caregiver should think twice before talking about his or her resident, co-workers, or others. The caregiver should remember that he or she does not always have access to the facts and that what he or she says can go a long way toward hurting the resident emotionally and tarnish the caregiving process.

A resident's records are also extremely important. Therefore, the caregiver should always keep a record of a resident's progress or lack of it. A resident's record should contain a multitude of information concerning his or her past, present and future personal life, medical and behavior patterns. The caregiver plays a vital role in keeping such information private and available only to those who are responsible for the resident's care including the family or designated family members or others involved in their welfare. Obviously, personal information about a resident must be kept confidential by the caregiver. Actually, if the caregiver considers how they would feel if they were a resident in someone's care and knew that everything about them was common knowledge, they would be much less likely to reveal the contents of a resident's record then such behavior might be curtailed. In reality, it is non-professional and could be considered abuse.

There is another important point to be remembered, and that is that a resident's record (and a matter of fact, the information and/

or record of anyone with knowledge of the resident) is considered to be legal evidence and can be used as such in judicial matters. Revealing anything about the resident or information contained in a record anywhere other than in the necessary course of care can do as much harm as ruthless gossip. Such behavior on the part of any caregiver is by law forbidden by the "privacy act" and every caregiver should know and adhere to the rules and regulations during the caregiving process.

THE RESIDENT'S FAMILY

The caregiver, if not a spouse, significant other, or family member, often sees the relatives of residents more frequently than any other individual in the community. Therefore, it is extremely important for the caregiver to understand the resident's family and what they mean to the resident. The caregiver has an important responsibility to record and share his or her observations of the resident with their families and the resident's reactions before and after interacting with the family, relatives, or others.

The resident's family often appears to be very difficult and trying to the caregiver. In the beginning, family members will often spend much time constantly questioning, making possible accusations, and becoming impatient with others and more specifically the caregiver regarding the resident. The reasons for this behavior are fairly simple: 1) the relatives feel guilty about having had to employ the services of others to care for their loved one. 2) They are afraid, because they do not understand the elderly, dementia or Alzheimer's disease. 3) They do not know how to behave. They feel altogether helpless, since they have been unable to handle the

72

problem at home and cannot seem to see their own part in the resident's illness and care.

Often, relatives are part of the problem as they in an attempt to help, break or refuse to adhere to treatment plans. For example, time after time, they will undo much of the work done by the caregiver. They will, in many instances, reward inappropriate behavior, breaking the rules of dieting, or out of their love and affection allow the resident to participate in activities, which have been restricted by the caregiver in activities of daily living. Such behavior on the part of the family always poses a problem and the caregiver should always use tact, patience, and understanding in dealing with such issues.

The caregiver's major responsibility to the resident's family is, of course, to take the best possible care of their loved one. Along with that basic duty, questions concerning the resident's illness should be referred to their physician or appropriate professional staff. Any discussion of the resident's behavior should be as limited as possible and appropriate professional personnel consulted. The best care of the resident includes the assurance that their personal possessions will be checked carefully as well as his or her grooming, toileting, dressing, dining and behavior. Much can be done by the caregiver by means of simple, quite, communication and reassurance. Telling the resident about a good meal a person ate the day before, his or her clothing, their likes and dislikes of clothing, music, art, sports, favorite songs, singing groups, television programs and outdoor projects, are all appropriate.

Relatives can be most useful in terms of providing a resident with small needed items such as a comb, brush, musical and art items, along with magazines which contain a lot of colorful pictures— outdoor scenes for men. For women, sewing, cooking and creative home projects, ideas such as books or approved items can be helpful in their habilitation. The caregiver can frequently form effective friendships with the family or relatives and can extend their duties and philosophy of caregiving through educational contact with them. Accepting monetary or special gifts from a family member or relative given expressly in the hope that the gift will ensure better or special treatment should never be done. Bridging the activities enjoyed by the resident during his or her life span should be continued and be defined early in the relationship between the caregiver and family members. In reality a comprehensive history should always be obtained before the caregiving duties begin. It makes the caregiving process much easier. It is productive and is more enjoyable in the resident's care. Appropriate music and art have been found to be most affective.

Accomplishing a task to meet the needs of a resident is extremely important to the caregiver by working through individuals best able to assist. The simplest way for the caregiver to get the things he or she needs, or to find out the things they want to know is first to consult with the person closest to the situation and to let him or her "take the situation" from there. When everyone who is caring for the resident knows what is going on, things generally run more smoothly during the resident's habilitation.

As a caregiver, we should separate as much as possible, our personal feelings from the job for the elderly man or woman who is old sick and tired with behavior problems associated with dementia or Alzheimer's disease. We as caregivers owe it to ourselves to try to forget our job as much as we can when we have a day off. It is a strenuous enough proposition to begin with, both mentally and physically, without carrying it home with us. To sum it all up, if the job means more to us than our paycheck; if it means the safety and the well being of our resident and the family as a whole, than we have assumed our obligations correctly. It is then that we are worthy of the tribute which is so rightly ours that we as caregivers are the arms, legs, and backbone of the caring and treatment process.

PERSONAL PROBLEMS AND THE CAREGIVER

As human beings, we all have personal problems—some are severe while some are dealing with problems of everyday living. Each of us needs to feel that someone is interested and cares about us. It is a given that a caregiver's role is a difficult one, and sometimes we have difficulties at home or in other personal areas in which we need some help or support. For example, a caregiver may have a marital, domestic, financial, religious, an illness with a spouse or difficulty with a child in school, a marriage or relationship problem. Then in addition, the caregiver could have an alcohol, drug with associated behavioral problems, which can have a negative impact on his or her ability to function appropriately. The important point here is that if he or she is going to continue to function in the role as a caregiver they must get professional help to resolve such problems or find another means of employment. There are far too many dangers that are hidden in such relationships. Most serious is the possibility that the caregiver with such personal problems will inflict their frustration on the resident for whom they are caring, and this should be avoided at all cost. The resident is, after all, an elderly sick person needing help, and most of the time is incapable of offering assistance with the caregiver's mental or emotional problems. Transferring problems to residents does not necessarily mean sitting down and telling a resident about their personal problems or difficulties. It is usually not as obvious. However, it is true that we do "take out our feelings" on our residents in a number of ways, and most of the time we are not aware of it. Under personal stress, and when we bring it to work, residents are sensitive and usually pick up our negative attitudes or hostility quickly which results in them exhibiting inappropriate behavior. For example, the caregiver may speak sharply or in a hostile manner to a resident. At times, they may force them to do or perform a task, which they do not wish to do, or when we are depressed around them, they feel our emotions and may become agitated. It is better if we stay home on a bad day or work out our problems in other ways such as taking a break, going for a walk, doing exercises. However, what is more meaningful is taking a hard and objective look at the resident and becoming aware of their age, their illness, and their needs. We should realize that they are someone's mother or father and that one day we will not be a caregiver but one of them—an old, sick man or woman with low self esteem, who feels unwanted, unloved and unappreciated. We only have to look at them and listen during which time our own feelings are usually resolved.

CHAPTER FIVE

COMMUNICATION AND
HUMAN RELATIONS

Every word that is spoken and every movement that is made between the caregiver and his or her resident sends a message to the other. Interpersonal communication is a transaction between the caregiver and the resident. In the Transactional Method of communication, the caregiver and the resident are both participating simultaneously. They mutually perceive each other, simultaneously listening to each other, and mutually engaged in the process of creating meaning in a therapeutic relationship.

In all interpersonal transactions, both the caregiver and resident bring certain preexisting conditions to the exchange that influences both the intended message and the way in which it is interpreted. Examples of these conditions include both the caregiver and the resident's value system. It is characterized by internalized attitudes and beliefs, culture and religion, social status, gender, background knowledge, experience, age and developmental levels. Finally, it includes the type of environment in which the communication takes place. It can be verbal, physical, gestural or a combination of all three methods.

Non-verbal expression is a primary communication system

in which meaning is assigned to various gestures and patterns of behavior. Some components of nonverbal communication include physical appearance and dress, body movement and posture, touch, facial expressions, eye behavior, and vocal cues or paralanguage. The meaning of each of these nonverbal components is culturally determined.

Active listening on the part of the caregiver is being attentive to what the resident is saying, through both verbal and nonverbal cues. Facilitative skills for attentive listening include sitting squarely in front of the resident, observing an open posture, leaning forward toward the resident, establishing eye contact, and relaxing.

Feedback is a method of communication for helping the resident consider a modification of his or her behavior. It is most useful when it is descriptive rather than evaluative. It is affective when it focuses on behavior rather than on the resident, is specific rather than general, is directed toward behavior that the resident can change, and imparts information rather than advice. The caregiver should be aware of the therapeutic or non-therapeutic value of the communication techniques used with the resident, as they are the "tools of psychological intervention."

Caregivers should be concerned with communication other than when the caregiver is involved in exceptional circumstances. Caregivers use communication skills or interpersonal skills every hour in the performance of their caregiving duties. In their work when providing caregiving services, the caregiver and resident listen to each other, notice what each other is doing, how they appear to be feeling, and how they talk to each other during the various levels of care. The use of communication skills differ from other relationship skills in that there is emphasis on attention to one person only—the resident, who may or may not be communicating to the best of their ability. Their thoughts and feelings both past and present may or may not be on a verbal basis. Therefore, the caregiver should put aside his or her own preoccupations and self-concerns in order to give full attention to the resident.

Communication is not a reciprocal relationship, which is based primarily on conversation; the focus is always on the resident. In ordinary everyday social contact, individuals are expected to share thoughts and feelings in varying degrees. Individuals give advice and help each other by relating to and identifying similarities in emotions or events that they have experienced. Their intention is to say, "I understand where you are coming from and you are not alone." The caregiver's aim is to comfort, to lessen the resident's physical, mental and emotional pain and feelings of alienation. While valuable in establishing social bonding, and interaction, along with integration, this kind of inter-actional discourse is valuable and important. However, it has its limits because the resident who is elderly with complex physical, mental and emotional problems cannot always express him or herself which inhibits the caregiver and his or her ability to interpret what the resident is trying to communicate. The fact that the resident is not always able to communicate his or her pain, or feelings and the caregiver is unable to process or interpret the results, often inhibits the caregiver from providing appropriate care.

There are some general principles, which the caregiver can apply in order to improve his or her skills of communication: they are: 1) "Know thyself." Although no caregiver could ever completely live up to this concept, it is possible for the caregiver to look at and examine more closely him or herself and at their relationships with others. It is not an easy task, but in the end, it becomes a highly rewarding experience. Through increased understanding of their own behavior, he or she is better equipped to understand the behavior of the resident for whom they are providing services.

The caregiver, in his or her relationships with residents might well ask him or herself these general questions: a) How do residents respond to me? b) What are my feelings about the elderly? c) What kind of judgments do I make about a resident? d) How do I react to these feelings and judgments? Moreover, e) Why do I particularly like or dislike certain residents? A therapeutic talk with one's self or over such questions with a co-worker, friend or relative will sometimes reveal valuable information, which the caregiver might not be capable of perceiving in themselves.

2) "Know the Resident". The caregiver should carefully observe the resident's behavior patterns—what they like to do and with whom, among others. The caregiver should also question the resident's physician and other professionals, about the resident's life before he or she began to function as a caregiver especially if they are caring for a resident who has dementia, Alzheimer's or a severe behavior problem. The caregiver may make it a point to meet the resident's family members or friends and assess the interaction-taking place. In addition, the caregiver may spend extra time with the resident, learning more about him or her through objective conversation.

VERBAL COMMUNICATION

The use of words and colloquialisms in such "objective conversations" with residents should be in accordance with the resident's capacity to understand. How words are expressed, has a definite effect on the attitude with which the resident receives them. There are all manner of ways in which a resident can be requested to do something! Such a request—regardless of whether it is firm, gentle, coaxing or humorous – will be well received by the resident if it is made with sincerity and with implied understanding.

SYMBOLIC AND LITERAL STATEMENTS

The caregiver often thinks that a very sick resident, at times, "talks a lot of nonsense". However, it is important for the caregiver to take everything and anything the resident says seriously. For example, a resident commented to a caregiver that there was a "wildcat" in her closet. The caregiver grinned and replied that it must be a vibration caused by the air conditioner and that it would be checked soon. Within the hour, the resident complained again that she had seen a "wildcat" in her closet. Finally, upon realizing that the resident was becoming quite agitated, the caregiver checked the resident's closet and sure enough, there was a small real life kitten in her closet. One of the volunteers who had used several pets during an activity program had left it behind. Therefore, it is difficult to judge sometimes what is fact and what is fiction. It is always wise to listen carefully and regardless of how ridiculous the complaint may sound, the caregiver should pursue the concern or complaint further.

NONVERBAL COMMUNICATION

From the minutely raised eyebrow of an individual, an athletic walk, or the influence of bodily movement, all have vast implications in the development of communication skills. Relatively speaking, interest in nonverbal communication, or bodily expression, has contributed largely to the study of human behavior by professionals in mental health during their therapeutic intervention, interviewing, counseling and psychotherapy. For the caregiver, it is particularly important. He or she may say one thing to a resident but feel another. For example, a caregiver may begin his or her caregiving duties and make initial contact with a male resident for whom he or she is caring. The caregiver notices that the resident is unshaven. His clothing is soiled with dried food particles, his hands are filthy and one of his arms is in a dirty sling. "Hello, John"! Says the caregiver. "You're looking fine today"! In reality, the caregiver is repulsed and is thinking, "You disgusting slob…Someone should have cleaned you up"! The caregiver has negative feelings toward the resident and is angry because he or someone in his family had not bathed, groomed and dressed him in clean clothing. The caregiver should realize that residents have an uncanny sensitivity to a caregiver's nonverbal expression. In the above example, the caregiver may "give him or herself away" in several ways. They may step back when they first look at the resident; they may put their hands in their pockets to keep from shaking hands with the resident, should the resident happen to extend such a greeting, or the caregiver's jaw may clench; he or she may frown; his or her voice may become loud. Although the resident may not know why, the resident will certainly sense that the caregiver is reacting in a negative manner and as a result feel insecure and ill at ease. It is generally much better for the resident if the caregiver would comfortably say: "John, why are you still having trouble with your arm?" "You will feel much better if you come along with me, and we will get you cleaned up!" Because the caregiver is, at the same time, telling the resident that he or she is messy, but that he or she cares enough about him as a resident to assist in cleaning him up. The caregiver is maintaining the resident's self-esteem and yet releasing the valve a bit on his or her feelings about the resident.

Positive nonverbal communication is perceived more easily. However, it is just as important that the caregiver be aware of positive bodily expressions as the caregiver seeks to overcome negative reactions, so he or she may seek to develop positive ones. It is of the utmost importance, however, for the caregiver to observe, report and attempt to understand the many nonverbal messages, which a resident conveys to them through their behavior.

In most instances, a resident's nonverbal communication is not that obvious. The caregiver should be aware of the subtle signs of increasing depression. For example, the puzzled expression of the resident who misidentifies someone, the self-abuse implied by constant pacing at night or the panic, which sometimes precedes a disturbed episode of inappropriate behavior, could all be signs of depression.

It is not difficult for a caregiver to develop a skilled awareness of body expressions and their meaning. A smile, frown, handshake, pat on the back, positive or negative shake of the head, gestures, crossed fingers and a multitude of other simple behaviors are all elements of communication. They have become such a vitally important facet of human communication that they can be observed easily wherever there are people.

All behavior is a form of communication is meaningful and can be interpreted with time and close observation. For example, when someone walks all night and sleeps during the day–what does that mean to the caregiver? It could very well mean the resident has a fear of losing his or her support system at night, having horrifying dreams or nightmares, being afraid of the dark, or afraid of dying. For the resident who complains constantly of a headache—could it be a toothache? These fears and others can be resolved if the caregiver remains alert, observant and communicates his or her observation to others. By being aware of such behavior as small and perhaps insufficient, as they may seem, if resolved, can prevent more serious episodes of behavior or illness later during the caregiving process. Such vital attention by the caregiver provides the resident with an environment which offers them numerous advantages—notably, security, and understanding—and one in which the resident's progress toward improved health and behavior can be accomplished more speedily.

Communication both verbal and nonverbal is vital to the caregiver and when done appropriately can reduce much of a resident's inappropriate behavior. The caregiver should always, when talking to a resident speak slowly, and clearly. One should never yell but should at times address the resident in a loud voice. If speaking in a loud voice has to be done often, the resident should be checked to see if he or she is hard of hearing. A caregiver should always use short sentences and use simple words, phrasing one thought in different ways if the resident does not seem to understand. Foreign accents can be difficult in understanding a conversation, therefore, the caregiver has to be patient, a good listener and assist a foreign resident by asking him or her to assist by repeating what they are trying to convey and by gesturing. At times, the caregiver will have to communicate with residents with brain damage and cognitive disorders who will respond to written word better than spoken which may be more effective if he or she writes a message. Others will sign to convey their comments. The caregiver must assume that the resident is capable of having, to some degree, insight that they do not remember. As a result, they should not speak or act around the resident as if he or she is not present. As a caregiver, we should construct our method of communication to match the residents. For example, if the resident can only answer yes or no, then ask only yes and no questions. Then, in addition, we should be an active listener. If we do not understand, we should say so and then ask him or her to repeat. If we still fail to understand, then guess what the resident is trying to say. In addition, we should use humor sarcasm very carefully because there are some residents who may not understand and may take what is said offensively. We should not forget that nonverbal communication is and can be more important than verbal. It can be extremely beneficial and useful if we use it in a reassuring manner. In doing so, we should always try to make eye contact. We can do so by facing the resident; touching, rubbing, feeling and stroking the resident's arms and hands are generally helpful. In addition, using gestures, pictures, and objects can help us improve comprehension of communication with the elderly.

Memory and orientation are generally always a problem when caring for the elderly. As caregivers, we have to develop creative and innovative methods and strategies do cope with such behavior. For instance, we can use clocks, pictures and calendars. Their confusion can be reduced if we are consistent, providing predictable routines. Repeating information and instructions is often helpful as well as keeping personal objects and belongings in the same place. Using simple directions is helpful. For example, if we want the resident to use the bathroom, we should tell him or her when they are near the bathroom rather than when the resident is leaving the dining area. We should always begin our conversation with the resident by first identifying the resident by stating his or her name and then identifying ourselves. This is especially true at night to reduce fear and confusion. Then, in addition, we should reduce competing stimulation such as a popular radio or television programming. Such permissive behavior on the part of the caregiver can interfere with the resident's ability to concentrate and can result in him or her exhibiting inappropriate behavior such as agitation.

Perhaps the one thing caregivers dread and find most difficult in the caregiving process is behavior problems. We must realize that inappropriate behavior must be interrupted quickly. We should redirect the resident from the situation, which is exciting him or her to a quiet area, and then in a calm and secure manner explain to the resident why we did this, using facts rather than guilt. When the resident is exhibiting inappropriate behavior, we should attempt to remove the resident from the situation redirecting his or her interest. Dementia and Alzheimer's residents are distractible because they have limited cognitive skills depending on the degree of their disease. We should make use of, take advantage of this, and remember that distraction and redirection are our most valuable communicative tools in dealing with this kind of behavior in these types of residents. However, we should not forget that isolation can lead to increased confusion, therefore, we should avoid using isolation alone to control their behavior—instead we should communicate and remain with them, giving them support. If, for example, when we find that the resident is non-receptive to our attention or communication we should leave him or her alone, keeping our distance but maintaining a watchful eye on them as their behavior can be and is often unpredictable. Instead, we should communicate to them that we understand why they want to be left alone and do not want to talk at this time and when they feel like talking, we will try again later.

If the resident is not cooperative, we should not force our demands or requests on them. Forcing a resident to do something against his or her will only increases the possibility of inappropriate and/or assaultive behavior. Instead, try again later, have another person, relative, family member or staff member try. Remember that the elderly with dementia or Alzheimer's disease are changeable in that their mood can and often changes very quickly and unexpectedly. When attempting to modify a resident's behavior we should treat successes and failures alike and maintain a chart or at least track his or her behavior of both appropriate and inappropriate, so that all family members and support groups can share and insure continuity and consistency in the resident's care. The resident should be treated with dignity and respect because increased self-esteem plays a positive role in reducing inappropriate or unacceptable behavior on the part of the resident.

There are times when we as caregivers want the resident to participate in an activity or go some place. When we do, we should approach the resident from the front and slowly reach out for his or her hand. We should communicate in a soft reassuring voice identifying ourselves and explaining to them what we are doing, where we are going and the reason for our decision, making every effort to reassure them. We should always avoid approaching the resident from behind or from his or her side, as this will most likely increase inappropriate and/or aggressive behavior on his or her part. Always approach the resident from the front.

The elderly have frequent episodes of sleep disorders. They are restless, some remain up all night, others wander about the home while others want the caregiver awake and with them at all times. We as caregivers should find ways to keep them awake and active during daylight hours. Such an effort will help them sleep at night. During the night, we should contribute to the resident's feelings of security and comfort by giving them back rubs, touching, feeling stroking and embracing them. Also keeping a night light on helps calm their fears.

Another issue, which is extremely important for the caregiver, is to be aware of their responses in caring for the elderly especially those with dementia or Alzheimer's disease. If we let our own emotions and responses show especially if they are negative then such behavior on our part as a caregiver can inflame and make our job even more difficult. Although human responses to frustration are normal, some common reactions on the part of the caregiver are inconsistent responses. If we exhibit such emotional responses as anger, hostility, fear, feelings of "why me, Lord" we tend to avoid or want to escape our responsibilities in providing sufficient care for the resident. Then, in addition, if we maintain a cold and distance approach in meeting the resident's emotional needs, we communicate rejection. Such mental and emotional feelings lead to a caregiver's fatigue, which interferes with the care the resident receives and the ability of the caregiver to provide adequate services and care.

As caregivers, we must realize that the elderly with dementia or Alzheimer's disease are extremely sensitive to our emotional state and reactions. As a result, they are likely to perceive our emotional responses as being directed to them, rather than to understand our spoken words. We must learn to put ourselves in the resident's situation and realize that one day we will be in the same or similar position. We have to constantly remind ourselves of this and of how we would want to be treated as a human being, who is old, sick and tired. We should always reinforce the resident's feelings of belonging. We can do so by using their name or a name they like each time we interact with them. We can reassure them that this is their home and that we are their friend. We can use gestures and touching as much as possible when appropriate. There are times when the resident may not understand our words but will be responsive to our touch, a pat on the back, or smile.

In summary, the caregiver should have or acquire good communication skills. Essentially, caregiving is concerned, or should be, with communication, yet clearly, it is different from other interpersonal exchanges. We use communication skills in some form every hour of every day when working with our residents. We listen to each other, notice what each other is doing, how we feel and we communicate with each other on various levels. The caregiver, however, should put aside his or her own personal preoccupations and self-concerns in order to give full attention to the resident. Communication for the caregiver is and will remain an important therapeutic tool to comfort, to lessen the resident's pain and feelings of alienation. Communication is of the utmost value in establishing social bonding and integration with the resident for whom we are caring in our role as a caregiver.

CHAPTER SIX

SPIRITUAL AND RELIGIOUS ISSUES

There are two areas in the life of the elderly, which the caregiver should realize that is of the utmost importance to the resident for whom they are caring. One is politics and the other is religion. Both are important issues but can be controversial, upsetting to the resident, and problematic to the caregiver. The best solution in coping with these topics is for the caregiver to be a good listener and agreeable with the resident's belief system. When the caregiver chooses to do otherwise it usually results in him or her becoming part of the problem rather than the solution.

Having said this a regular spiritual practice, a religious belief system and church affiliation is important to the elderly and can provide structure and a sense of peacefulness during late life. The elderly and their religious connection seems to provide them with tangible mental and emotional benefits which gives them a sense of hope and a sense of well being which can help them cope with the multiple and at times complex issues of living.

Recent research conducted on how the elderly with dementia and Alzheimer's disease cope with these issues revealed that the strongest predictors of mental and emotional strength were not the frequency with which individuals attended formal church services but rather it was the inner strength and support they possessed from their spiritual beliefs. The research also revealed that the elderly who were involved in church and religious activities had higher levels of well being, fewer episodes of depression as well as fewer incidences of suicide and cognitive difficulties. The studies further revealed that the elderly who were active participants in religious services showed improved overall emotional, well being, including increased optimism and less depressive reactions. They also had stronger social support systems and fewer unhealthy behaviors and methods of coping with life's issues. It is not unusual for elderly residents in nursing homes to express their religious or spiritual views in the following manner. "At my age and with my health problems I don't attend church outside the facility any more. However, my church friends still visit me and this helps. My faith means the most to me. I am comforted because I know that there is a life beyond death. I know that I will see my deceased husband and friends again. My faith is stronger and more meaningful than ever".

According to existing data, there is nothing more important to the elderly than their religion or spirituality. It seems that their religious belief system helps them in their failure and keeps them steady in success. It appears that their spirituality makes their life satisfying and promises them a life to come. Their religious faith permits them to discover themselves and find their place in life, to be successfully married, make good parents, perform their jobs in life, get their satisfaction in doing the right things and face death in a calm, confident and positive manner. The elderly considers that there is nothing else in their life that motivates them than to accomplish the elements of life except religion or spirituality.

When defining Christianity or what it means to be religious the elderly, for the most part, has similar opinions. The first opinion is to be religious means to believe in God and to take Him seriously in their lives. It should be noted, however, that there are two elements in this definition. There is the belief in God, but that is not all. One who believes in God but does nothing about it is not religious. He or she must work out their belief system in practical ways in his or her life and in the support of God's work in the world.

On the other hand, the second opinion expressed by the elderly, is that one must support works that might have God's approval and not believing in God is equally unsatisfactory. This second part of the definition, which defines what they believe, mandates that for one to be religious they must do God's work because he or she believes in God, and for God's sake. They believe that this ties earth and Heaven together, and that the religious man or woman lives in both realms, the physical and the spiritual. They believe that the physical is really the manifestation of the spiritual and so he or she orders their physical life under spiritual control. Most seem comfortable with this concept and understanding of their religious beliefs in life.

The caregiver must be sensitive to any and all concepts of religious beliefs. They must realize that there is no single concept of "normal" that applies across all persons, situations and cultures. Mainstream concepts of caregiving must be expanded to incorporate the religious and spiritual dimensions, which influence the lives of those brought up in other religious denominations and cultures. The caregiver must be flexible and maintain a respectful attitude towards other therapeutic values, beliefs and traditions. The caregiver must assume that their own view of reality is culturally based. Caregiving theories have been developed from Caucasian western caregivers (mainly European and American), inextricably influenced by Judeo-Christian morality. Ideas of morality formed by religious belief may differ between the majority culture and minority cultures.

In caring for the elderly who are, for the most part, old, sick and at times suffer from complex mental and emotional disorders as well as dementia and Alzheimer's disease, should realize that the resident usually brings up religious and spiritual concerns. The themes should be considered and taken seriously by the caregiver because they are of importance and meaningful to the resident. The themes, which are generally brought up by the resident consist of the following:

1. Spirituality, religion, practices and traditions.
2. Morality, moral values teaching, sin and evil.
3. Life-guiding values.
4. A perception of God or a higher power.
5. A search for spiritual health.
6. Religious affiliation, vocation, a call.

Before beginning the caregiving process, the caregiver should take and review the resident's religious history. The history should include the following:

1. Past and present religious as well as spiritual information.
2. Role of religion during his or her childhood, adolescence and adulthood.
3. Involvement in church activities, organized religion, church membership, attendance, devotion, loyalty and commitment.
4. Effects, impact of religious faith on his or her activities, decisions, lifestyle, relationships, and especially "mixed marriages."

The history should contain concerns related to a loss or questioning of faith, such as:

1. The differences, conflicts, problems with a church, organized religion, teachings, ministers, authority, inappropriate behavior, biblical leaders, secular, e.g., hypocrisy.
2. Effects of suffering, losses, disillusionment of faith.
3. Effects of chemical dependency on religious beliefs and practices.

The caregiver should also include the following in his or her religious history regarding the resident's concerns about or related to conversion to a different faith:

1. Being considered apostate, unchurched or lost by previous faith.
2. Marriage, and the rearing of children in a particular denomination.
3. The initiation into a new religious body.
4. Ceremonies and holidays of a particular denomination.
5. Relationships with his or her family of origin.

One's religion and/or spirituality is a private matter of which the caregiver must respect regardless of his or her own belief system. The life of a caregiver is much like religion – Complex. Some is nice and comforting while some is not but is like life, all of it is fascinating. Caregivers who want to survive over the long haul must never lose their wonder at the unpredictability and uniqueness of the human condition. Caregivers, for their sakes and those of others, must love life and bring that love to others especially the elderly. That, of course, means appreciating the full range of human emotions including religious values of the elderly who are in our care.

The author included religious and/or spiritual issues for

discussion for two fundamental reasons. First, the author wanted to highlight the fact that from the world's religious or spiritual perspective, caregiving is a sacred art, and at times a final ritual, the last opportunity we have to discover life's ultimate meaning and purpose of life. Therefore, religious traditions should remind us as caregivers of the importance of life, and that whatever lies on the other side of death is as real, if not infinitely more so, than life itself to our residents. These rituals offer caregivers and residents alike a sense of hope. Second, I wanted to emphasize that caregiving is a sacred art--one of love for the caregiver in both theory and practice. In fact, living itself is an art and that if we want, as a caregiver, to learn how to live and love we should proceed in the same way we would if we wanted to learn any other art form in life.

Religious orders have always been in the forefront of caregiving. The art of caregiving has deep roots in the spiritual traditions of both east and west. Shakyamuni Buddha instructed his followers to attend to the suffering of others. Five centuries later, Jesus taught the same message. Both practiced what they preached by directly caring for the sick and elderly.

Caregiving is difficult. Discipline is required on the caregiver's part if he or she is to adequately cope with a resident's problems. Without discipline, we can solve nothing. The caregiver can acquire such discipline and succeed as a caregiver if he or she makes and adheres to the following choices so eloquently pinned by Father Norbert Weber, M.S.C. and quoted in three minutes a day by Father John Catoir, Director of the Christophers:

- Choose to love rather than hate.
- Choose to smile rather than frown.
- Choose to build rather than destroy.
- Choose to persevere rather than quit.

- Choose to praise rather than gossip.
- Choose to heal rather than wound.
- Choose to give rather than grasp.
- Choose to act rather than delay.
- Choose to forgive rather than curse.
- Choose to do unto others, as you would have them do unto you.

CHAPTER SEVEN

MANAGING BEHAVIOR

In caring for an elderly resident inappropriate behavior is always problematic as it interferes with the caregiver's ability to adequately care for the multi-faceted needs of the resident for whom he or she is providing care. Although behavior problems must be addressed, there has been far too much focus placed on classifications of the residents physical, mental, emotional and spiritual maladaptive behaviors. That is, care plans have been designed according to a pattern of specific diseases and associated behaviors—their causes, symptoms, treatment and outcome which is at times too demanding for the caregiver. In many respects this has been extremely damaging, since it results in two things: 1) It produces a tendency to lump all residents into a specific classification—with a diagnostic title—thus resulting in the resident losing his or her individuality and state of being, and 2) it leaves out much of the understanding of basic personality needs which are so important for caregivers to know. Since all elderly residents differ, as does their reactions to their illness, it is much more important to understand the reasons for their inappropriate behavior than it is to know a particular diagnosis or any of the many other titles of classifications. Many residents in our care exhibit a number of different symptoms, which could fit into any one of the various types of illnesses and by no means follow a set of routine patterns. Classifications generally should only be used as a guide or as a means of communication for the caregiver. The caregiver gets a general idea of inappropriate behaviors and their patterns from the "titles" or the "diagnosis." However, general ideas are not enough! It is important that the caregiver in particular, (since he or she is the one who has to contend with a resident's maladaptive behavior twenty-four hours a day), know and understand behavior problems in detail so that he or she can handle them adequately.

For simplicity, behavior patterns have been grouped under thirteen general headings by the author. However, it is absolutely necessary for the caregiver to keep in mind at all times that his or her residents are ill. Some have severe physical illnesses or injuries while others may have dementia, a psychiatric or behavior disorder, or a combination of these problems. All residents are unpredictable. No resident will behave in an exact manner in any given situation, and it is for this reason that the caregiver needs to develop an acute awareness of the behavior of human beings, including him or herself as a caregiver.

1. Over-activity (hyperactivity disorder) indicates intense activity, usually without a sense of direction. It can be verbal, motor or both, and is not confined to any one type of resident. In fact, any resident can become overactive, depending on a given situation, circumstance, and his or her reaction to it. This is especially true when over-activity is mentioned or observed by those who are unfamiliar with such behavior. Their initial impression is usually a negative one. They often picture the resident as being menacing, angry, destructive and even homicidal. This, of course, is not the case, and inexperienced caregivers working for the first time with

the elderly resident, especially those with Alzheimer's dementia are surprised at the small number of residents whose illness manifests itself in this negative fashion. There are, for example, residents who talk, sing, and write profusely all day and sometimes all night. Some if allowed, make beds, scrub floors and walls, clean toilets, and so on indefinitely. Others walk, run, dance, and are seemingly never still. In addition, a few are angrily overactive and destroy objects, pick fights and attempt to harm him, herself, or others. One thing is certain, however, and that is that over-activity of any kind demands and should receive attention from the caregiver. It is well to note here, however, that many caregivers fall into the trap of giving most of their attention to those residents who are overactive leaving the quite, underactive residents alone to look after themselves. There are some good reasons for this. For one thing, as mentioned previously, the overactive resident demands attention. For another, the overactive resident is usually more "interesting" and "amusing" than the quite ones. Still another reason is that it is easier to establish a relationship with an overactive resident, since communication is forthcoming whether it is wanted or not! However, these things do not mean that the overactive resident needs more care. All kinds of residents should have as much care as the caregiver can provide.

One can always find a stimulus for overactivity. Although many times the reasons are subtle and difficult to define. The stimulus may be a very realistic one, such as a visit of a disliked relative, loud music, a high wind, loud and unacceptable discussions, or annoying noises. It may also be emotional. For instance, the guilt feelings of a resident who is driven to walk, scrub, sweep or clean all day or night may have a severe emotional problem. Others can agitate the resident into causing a disturbance of other kinds of inappropriate behavior. They can become upset when threatened by an activity, which has not been adequately explained to them. Frequently, inappropriate behavior is the result of fear, loneliness or both. If the caregiver examines the situation thoughtfully and thoroughly he or she may find anger as being the real basis for the resident's aggressive behavior. Many times it may seem that anger is a mask assumed by the resident resulting in him or her shouting, walking up and down his or her living area, becoming troublesome to the caregiver and others providing or receiving care.

What can we do as caregivers about the overactive resident? He or she disturbs others, upsets routine care, and often frightens others. They can be a problem to themselves in terms of their physical well-being, may be destructive of his or herself, and of others' personal property, as well as being considered a management problem. There are no set rules for handling these kinds of residents who exhibit these kinds of behavior. There is no one-two-three routine, no particular number of personnel who should be involved, no special "holds" that can be routinely used. Behavioral plans can and should be developed individually for each individual resident based on their behavior patterns. Also behavioral plans to control a resident's behavior should take into consideration the size of the resident, age, and the degree of his or her mental, emotional and physical behavior. The reason for the behavior exhibited must be considered. For example, when and where it occurs, the attitude of the caregiver, whether or not his or her physician is present or approves of behavior procedures implemented. All are important factors. Also, whether or not the resident is under the influence of medication or other mind altering substances is extremely important and all of these elements depend on the kind of Behavior Plan that is written.

Each situation demands its own special plan of treatment and everyone will differ. However, there are some important generalities, which will apply. First of all, inappropriate behavior on the part of a resident does not need to occur as often as it does. In other words, when a caregiver knows his or her resident well he or she senses when an unacceptable behavioral incident is going to occur, often knowing why and can follow the steps in the resident's plan of treatment plan to prevent it.

Example of Behavioral Treatment Plan

Problem: Combativeness – hitting, slapping, striking others.

Goal: To reduce resident's combative behavior.

Objective: Will have less than three (3) episodes of physically abusive behavior per week.

Strategies: Remove from area. Reward all positive behavior using verbal, gestural and physical prompts along with approved food and drinks.

Steps:

1. Approach the resident in a calm manner.
2. Speak in a calm but firm voice; make eye contact.
3. Calmly explain reason for intervention.
4. Slowly position self on left side of resident.
5. Lock right arm in left arm of resident; walk away from area.
6. Redirect to private area; calm by talking, touch and stroking.
7. Perform breathing exercises with resident to calm.
8. When calm, return to original place of activity.

9. Repeat steps as often as necessary, rewarding all positive behavior.

In addition to the above steps, the resident should be encouraged to participate in activities of his or her choice to decrease energy level. Also, the resident should be encouraged to discuss his or her thoughts on why inappropriate behavior was exhibited. The family should be involved in treatment plan when they are available.

However, not all incidents of unacceptable behavior are obvious especially in the beginning. It takes a while for the caregiver to get to know and understand his or her resident, just as it takes time to bond or form any friendship. Therefore, an outburst of inappropriate behavior can occur without warning, and the problem becomes urgent, in need of an immediate solution. This is why it is vital to define a resident's individual strength, weaknesses and needs as quickly as possible and develop a treatment plan to deal with inappropriate episodes of behavior or develop a strategy to cope with unacceptable episodes of behavior as they occur. Family members are an excellent resource to help us as caregivers define such incidents during our early interaction with the resident making our job more productive and providing the resident an opportunity to experience an improved quality of life.

Another method a caregiver can use for the overactive resident is work with him or her in a calm quite manner. This approach can do more to help the resident than all the orders or coercion given by anyone. Such an attitude is futile only when a resident has completely lost control, which seldom happens.

A third general principle is applicable when a resident is overactive and this is diversion. Diversion for the overactive resident can be more specific. For example, open-air activity, if the resident is able and the weather permits, allows a resident to work off much excess energy that might otherwise be spent in a problematical manner. Walks and other simple activities can be developed to assist the resident's over-activity in almost any situation. Helping with cleaning their living area, bed making, sorting linen, mopping and sweeping their living area, are all energy-ridding activities. Sometimes residents who write or draw at great length can be interested in making posters, composing artwork, song lyrics, or copying magazine articles. Incidentally, one can get many clues to the reasons for underlying overactive behavior by reading some of the material that these busy residents who draw or write produce.

The fourth and final general principle for the caregiver to remember in the management of the overactive resident is that someone should stay with them as much as possible. Among other observations, it is extremely important to note the physical appearance of the resident, for overactive residents frequently develop physical conditions, which require attention. If there is evidence of abnormal physical signs such as fever, flushing, rapid pulse, bright eyes, etc. then these symptoms should be brought to the attention of a professional. There are times when an overactive resident neglects to eat and drink enough fluids, and they become dehydrated or develop faulty elimination. Their skin may break down—usually first characterized by redness and swelling. All of these things are as much the caregiver's responsibility as is the resident's mental, emotional and spiritual stability.

One final comment on the management of the overactive resident should be recognized. The author wishes to state the carefully considered opinion that the use of mechanical restraints is never "proper" or acceptable and demonstrates only a lack of knowledge of something else to control aggressive behavior other than mechanical restraints. Mechanical restraints only increases management problems, for, no matter how well administrated or how well supervised, it can do no more than increase fear, tension, anger, suspicion, and frustration in an already disturbed resident. The caregiver should always, when confronted with behavior problems, consult a professional trained in behavior modification techniques to develop a behavior plan, which extinguishes inappropriate behavior and promotes appropriate behavior.

2. Under-activity (hypo activity disorder). In many instances, the under-active resident presents a much more serious problem to the caregiver than does the overactive resident. These are the ones who seemingly do not want attention, who, at any rate, do not make their desires, or needs known, whose whole world has slowed down or for the most part stopped. They are depressed, feel unwanted, lonely, often suicidal, and are filled with a mental and emotional anguish so great that it seems to be impenetrable both to the resident and to the caregiver. These are the ones who sit or lie down all day, and through the night, and apparently live in a world that has little of any meaning. Actually, much seethes in their minds, and their needs are many. Besides the things that these residents want, there are things that they do not want. However, the uncontrollable listlessness makes it impossible for them to make these needs and desires known.

There are three general types of under-activity present in the elderly resident. First, there is the resident who cooperates with the caregiver and the demands and routines made on them. For example, this type of resident eats, sleeps, and bathes regularly but otherwise wishes to be left alone not wanting to participate in activities and does not interact with others. Secondly, there is the resident who is profoundly depressed, who does not want to eat, bathe, groom him or herself or even be disturbed. At times these residents become negativistic; that is, they balk at every activity afforded them refusing to cooperate on any level and sometimes even doing the opposite of what is requested of them. They often sit, day after day, hour after hour daydreaming or staring into space, curled up in bed in their room isolated from others. And, thirdly, there is the resident who is bedfast because of one or more physical problems which incapacitates him or her, and has to participate in an under-active role, although not always by choice.

In addition, problems arise for the caregiver who works with the under-active resident. Physical problems experienced by the resident become most important because it is visible. Careful observation and recording must be made of the amount of food and liquid intake, the amount of sleep, the regularity or irregularity of elimination and the condition of the resident's skin. If the caregiver constantly keeps in mind the fact that all normal human processes are considerably slowed down with this kind of behavior, he or she realizes the serious consequences that may follow. Residents may become seriously undernourished and dehydrated, therefore, lowering their resistance to disease and becoming easy prey for infectious illnesses. The problems of feeding such residents and what to do about them are issues with which the caregiver has to cope requiring patience and meticulous attention in that every effort should be expanded to assist the resident to eat. Emotional fatigue is not conducive to sleep and, in fact, may foster wakefulness in the resident. The resident who expends little, if any energy is likely to lie awake hours on end at night and it is important that the caregiver make sure whether his or her resident is getting enough quality sleep. A still form lying in bed does not mean that he or she is sleeping. For example, a resident who sleeps normally breathes differently and usually will stir a little when approached by the caregiver at night with a light. The resident who is depressed will often retain their products of elimination and should be encouraged to go to the toilet on a regular basis. Severe obstruction can result in a resident who is neglected concerning elimination requiring medical intervention. These are such issues in which the caregiver must be aware of and we never know when such issues will arise. For example, a caregiver has a female resident who is almost completely negativistic and refuses to communicate her feelings or needs. The resident never talked, and often would stay in her room all the time resisting any and all efforts to encourage her to participate in any of the activities of daily living including toileting. However, the amazing thing was that every four or five days she would approach willingly the caregiver and say, "I need an enema". In addition, during the process she would cooperate totally without any resistance.

This illustrates two vital points in which the caregiver should know or at least be aware of. They are:

1) That the resident had to keep track of her own problems of elimination, and

2) That the resident was actually in very good contact with her environment, the caregiver and other people in it, even though she was apparently non-communicative. It is essential for the caregiver to remember that many under-active residents are fully aware of what goes on around them. For this reason, it is important for the caregiver to use good judgment of what is said and done in the resident's presence. There are numerous documented instances where the resident has remembered things that happened to them, and around them when, to all appearances, the resident was

completely oblivious to what the caregiver said or did while in their care.

A resident's skin care is another vital area in which the caregiver must always be aware of when caring for the under-active resident. For the most part activity and stimulation of the body parts can prevent care to areas which are affected. The caregiver should be aware that the resident's legs, shoulder blades and lower back are most frequently affected and that frequent medicated rubs and the application of a soft powder can do much to prevent the development of the much more difficult problem of bedsores. In addition, a resident should be turned frequently, kept dry, clean and should have their bed linen changed and straightened frequently.

For the resident who is out of bed but severely under-active, short walks, simple rhythmic dance steps, and rest with legs and feet elevated help to eliminate ulcers. Once a resident has been allowed to contract a circulatory ulcer of a lower leg, it is usually difficult to cure. In addition, if the resident remains under-active, even though it may heal periodically, it can break down again. This is why the under-active resident should have his or her legs massaged several times each day.

The caregiver should realize that these things are at times difficult to accomplish, because the under-active resident does not want to move and they resent being encouraged to participate in such a needed activity. They often become quite hostile if the caregiver is insistent that they participate making the caregiver's job even more difficult. Even though it may well be understood that the resident wants to be left alone, it is still important for the caregiver to find a way of motivating the resident to participate. The question is often raised by caregivers as to why residents become withdrawn and antisocial. They also wonder how they can help the resident return to normal socialization. Many residents withdraw because of the image they have of themselves, low self-esteem, poor motivation, or as most call "self-pity". Somehow, they feel that they have failed in life and have been rejected by those whom they hold most closely or lovingly; they simple withdraw, are depressed and have frequent crying episodes as a result. It is difficult, however, to convince this kind of depressed resident that it takes more action than words to convince him or her that other people do like them, want and desire to interact with them on a social basis— that they want to be their friend. This is not an easy task for the caregiver. It is a slow, painstaking process, requiring a genuine liking, and interest in the resident, as well as faith in his or her ability to respond to the caregiver's intervention in resolving their inappropriate behavior. Other residents may feel extremely guilty about things which happened in their past, imaginary or otherwise and will constantly blame themselves, particularly in their own reasoning or mindset. This is usually a deeper problem in which a professionally trained individual can do most for the resident. The caregiver should refrain from projecting their own personal judgment, moral opinions or belief system onto the resident. When done, the caregiver becomes part of the problem rather than the solution. When the caregiver makes a referral or shares such information with the resident's personal physician or healthcare provider he or she displays respect for and thoughtfulness about his or her resident, not allowing him or herself to increase the resident's guilt intentionally. Still other residents cannot readily account for their feelings of grief, depression and need a willing and listening ear. In this case, the caregiver should usually be a good listener rather than an interpreter. The resident is, when talking about sensitive occurrences in their lives, trying to work through the reasons for their feelings of listlessness and apathy and want to talk to someone in the hope that they might discover the root cause of their problem.

In the final analysis, one more suggestion is made which applies to both the overactive and under-active resident, in fact, to any resident. Sometimes, it is wise to avoid forcing the issue when a realistic number of attempts have been made. Usually, in due time, a resident will cooperate and do what is asked of him or her, but there are times, as with all residents, when he or she has to be "in the mood". For example, a young caregiver, inexperienced in dealing with residents with mental problems, kept insisting that the elderly woman for whom she was caring take her shower. The resident insisted on having a bath in the tub instead, insisting that she was Queen Cleopatra and royalty did not take showers like ordinary women. The more the caregiver persisted, the angrier the resident became. Finally, she turned on the caregiver and gave her a scary stare but luckily was not aggressive. A caregiver should know that if she had made known, once, what she wanted, the resident, taking her own time, would have most likely wandered into the shower and accomplished the task of taking a shower on her own without controversy.

Therefore, routine-ness should not become all-powerful. There is a tendency, at times, for caregivers to put order and cleanliness above the personal needs of the resident. Although order and cleanliness are an important aspect of life, there are times when they can be postponed in favor of activities for residents, which contribute to their emotional well-being. Most of us who serve as caregivers have had the experience of visiting homes and facilities where the floors shined, beds made, furniture appropriately placed looking as though the room had never been occupied. The resident sat idly in a chair, often afraid to move, or were so dysfunctional that they were secluded. Not even a card table, television set, radio, magazines were available in their room since they might appear disorderly. A comfortably disordered room might not impress important visitors, but the caregiver finds a happier resident in such an environment.

REGRESSION

Regression in a resident can be a most troubling problem because it involves feelings of disgust and impatience on the part of the caregiver. These feelings of disgust and impatience can be so offensive to the caregiver that such behavior on the part of the resident often interferes with his or her ability to work affectively with the resident. Caregivers often cannot or will not work with a resident whose behavior has regressed to the point of being child-like in the areas of activities of daily living. For example, many sick residents have regressed to the point where they urinate on the floor, soil themselves, smear the products of elimination, eat with their hands, become overly affectionate, exhibit inappropriate sexual acts, and are not at all interested in the usual, normal activities of life. All of these behaviors are not only disturbing to the caregiver but also to others with whom they interact.

Many caregivers wander why these residents revert to this type of infantile behavior. However, when working with the elderly the caregiver should realize that many of their elderly residents suffer from Alzheimer's dementia and as a result, they lose many of the skills of activities of daily living. These elderly residents are in the process of completing the "cycle of life" during which time they revert to childhood behavior. The difference between the behavior of a child and the elderly is that the child is learning and growing out of their infantile behavior. On the other hand, the elderly, especially those with Alzheimer's disease, are losing skills once learned and begin to regress to child-like behavior, which includes exhibiting certain pleasurable sensations connected with eating, elimination and sexual activity.

In order for the caregiver to help a resident learn, unlearn, or relearn lost skills in their activities of daily living, it is necessary to assist them by developing behavioral plans. The behavior plan should define what task is needed to be taught and then the task should be broken down into small simple steps beginning the process with verbal, gestural, and physical prompting. When an assigned task is performed appropriately, the resident should be rewarded by giving him or her verbal, edible food or drinks until he or she can perform the task independently.

LOSS

The caregiver should accept the basic fact that we all experience loss in life. Accepting this fact is helpful to the caregiver in understanding loss and knowing how to respond effectively to it. Loss happens. Loss is a part of life. When the caregiver accepts that, they can use the energy that they would spend hoping that it does not happen to them as caregivers, to deal with their resident's loss in a supportive and nonjudgmental way.

GRIEF

The goal of the caregiver in helping the resident resolve his or her grief is to gradually detach enough from his or her loss so they can form new and life-giving attachments with other people, places and things. Grief is a normal response to a particular loss of friends, family or significant other, place or object. It does not equal depression. A depressed person often develops guilt, self-blame and unrealistic feelings responsible for their loss. A grief stricken person, on the other hand, may wish that they had done something different, but do not persistently blame him or herself.

Grief is not to completely let go of the person, thing, and situation or object that has been lost. What once was lives on in one's memory. When a resident reattaches him or herself to others and to things, it means that what was is no longer the dominant concern in one's life. However, what was never and should not go away. Therefore, the primary goal of grief is to embrace what is and that will be in the future without having to completely separate from what has been in the past.

DEATH

The caregiver must be capable of supporting the resident who grieves over a variety of death situations. All losses, especially the death of a parent, spouse, child, relative or significant other can be a significant and life-altering experience. The finality of death can make such a loss devastating. Many factors affect the journey of grief following a death of a loved one. The manner of death, the degree to which it was anticipated, and how close the survivor was to the deceased are but a few of the issues affecting grief after death. One key factor affecting the journey of grief following death is the kind of relationship that existed between the resident and the deceased. The resident may have many deep questions, both spoken and unspoken about death. Why did this happen to me? How does it affect my belief in God? Can I hope for a miracle? What happens after death? Caregivers should not rush in with their own answers and opinions. Instead, they can affirm the vital importance of such inquiries by listening intently giving the resident their full attention in a sincere interesting manner. The caregiver should try to establish with the resident an intimate relationship of mutual respect and trust. Sitting and listening without judging without over reacting, noting what is said and what is left unsaid seeking a way to understand helps the resident to comprehend, process, and understand such an important event in their life.

ADDICTION

Addiction requires attention from the caregiver because the behavior manifested by the resident exhibiting these particular behaviors has long been considered comparatively normal and generally accepted by society at least until recently. Strictly defined, addiction means complete dependence on a drug or alcohol wherein the resident will go to any lengths to obtain the desired substance. Actually, one can become addicted to many things which society writes off as "habit" such as cigarettes, foods, sweets, non-alcoholic beverages, sex and even people and body parts. Certainly, when a resident persistently pursues something or someone that is harmful to him or herself, they can legitimately be called "addicted." Therefore, the caregiver should remember that such addictions are important symptoms, which may be indicative of a more serious illness or behavior. Therefore, the caregiver should maintain certain fundamental attitudes that will be helpful. They are:

1) Be nonjudgmental.
2) Maintain a heightened awareness.

3) Have a philosophy of providing holistic care.
4) Provide concern for overall well-being of resident.

SEXUAL PROBLEMS

There will be times when the caregiver will have to deal with sexual issues, i.e., arousal, aversion, desire, dysfunction, masochism, pain, sadism with the most prevalent being masturbation, homosexual activity, consensual sexual relations and privacy issues. This can be extremely problematical to the caregiver. However, the caregiver should remember that these types of sexual experiences are not an illness or the cause of the resident's need for care. At no time should the caregiver be critical of or amused at such behavior. It is well to remember always that it is easier to criticize than try to be patient, listen, observe, understand, be attentive and report concerns of such behavior to responsible family members and medical personnel who are involved.

ANXIETY DISORDERS

This type of resident is not able to make a healthy compromise with his or her conflicts and whose resulting anxiety needs to be converted into various physical complaints or compulsive, ritualistic behavior. Unlike the psychotic, he or she does not escape into a world of unreality. In general, a resident who has an anxiety disorder is generally presentable looking, takes care of many of his or her own personal needs, joins in social events without much prodding and is relatively easy for the caregiver to persuade to cooperate. The outward behavior revolves mostly around tension, evidenced by pacing, increased perspiration, lack of appetite and an inability to sleep adequately. The three greatest problems with which the caregiver has to cope are 1) taking their prescribed medication. These residents either want "pills" all the time, refuse to take them, or hoard their medication—some for the purposes of suicide; 2) the resident makes repetitive complaints to which the caregiver has to listen to patiently, day in and day out, and, 3) the patients apparent inability to help him or herself for which only the development of a profound degree of patience can be a panacea for the caregiver.

PERSONALITY DISORDERS

Of all inappropriate behavior exhibited by a resident for which a caregiver is responsible, it is an antisocial disorder. These residents were once called "psychopaths" and later "sociopaths". These individuals tend to be dramatic, emotionally unstable, seek an over abundance of attention, their moods are often frequent but shallow. They often have an intense amount of interpersonal conflicts both individually and collectively. Because of their tendency to ignore conformity of anything, they often influence others to exhibit dysfunctional behavior. They seem incapable of forming any motivation to change. No other behavior tests the caregiver's intelligence, patience, and moral self-defense, as does this disorder. However, there are a few suggestions concerning the management of such residents that can be utilized without difficulty if the total picture of the resident's behavior is grasped calmly and with some degree of clarity. They are:

1) Be consistent and firm.
2) Be reserved. Never become emotionally involved with them.

3) Limit trust.

4) Keep the resident busy.

COGNITIVE DISABILITIES

The caregiver should deal with the mentally challenged resident in terms of the degree of their abilities. Tolerant and understanding their supervision is a most important part of their total care. Although cognitive disability is a baffling, sometimes depressing and often frustrating problem to the caregiver, it should always be handled with kindness, patience and an innate capacity to develop whatever potential skills the individual may have.

RELIGIOUS ISSUES

Religious convictions is an extremely personal matter with most residents and in many instances, if discussed in depth with a resident may result in initiating emotionally charged feelings and emotions. Religion is one of the strongest influences in human life containing needs both mental and emotional, which must be met. The caregiver often has to deal with a resident who is elderly, sick and often suffering from a terminal illness who naturally has many deep, unresolved, and complicated questions, both spoken, and unspoken, regarding religious issues. However, caregivers should never rush into the residents need to discuss religion with their own answers and opinions. The caregiver should instead affirm the importance of the resident's comments regarding their beliefs by listening intently and establishing with them an intimate relationship of mutual respect and trust regarding the resident's religious convictions. The caregiver should never over-react but instead listen in attentive silence, and just go where they go. The caregiver should accept the resident's way as if it were their own, listening without being judgmental and without reacting noting what is said and what is left unsaid. The caregiver should only seek to understand rather than attempting to impose his or her own religious beliefs on the resident. The caregiver should maintain a passive posture when discussing religion. Such a position will help both the caregiver as well as the resident.

THE CAREGIVER'S ANXIETY

It is a normal reaction for the caregiver to feel anxious at the thought of being responsible for another person, especially his or her behavior, which is at times aggressive and difficult to understand. It is not surprising that the caregiver may feel overwhelmed when assuming his or her responsibility for the care and well-being of an elderly person who is experiencing a number of serious and complex needs in life. His or her anxiety can cause a collision with the resident by intervening with a change of a subject or promoting a positive attitude towards life. Anxiety is often linked to impossible expectations of oneself as a caregiver. Therefore, caregivers need to assess their experience and training and accept their limitations. The caregiver will actually do the resident an injustice if they attempt to work at levels beyond their experience and capabilities. However, it may be appropriate when the caregiver is closely supervised. There are times when the residents will, at times, not only be elderly, but will also exhibit psychotic behavior and the caregiver's functioning is likely to be impeded by their "self-talk" or thoughts during the caregiving process. The caregiver often raises the following questions regarding his or her capabilities. 1)

Will I, "through the caregiving process, be able to give them a sense of self-worth and save them." 2) "Will I be personally responsible if the resident takes his or her life?" 3) If I am a competent caregiver, "will I be able to persuade them to change their behavior"?

These kinds of self-statements are not realistic. The caregiver should examine any irrational beliefs they might have on the subject of his or her caregiving responsibilities toward the residents who exhibit such behavior and replace them with ones taking into account the residents responsibilities and choice. All inappropriate behavior regarding their safety should be taken seriously. The resident's behavior may be cries for help or they may equally be considered decisions that the caregiver has made having weighed all the pros and cons of the resident's life situations.

Some of the reasons for such behavior on the part of the resident may be:

1) Painful emotions such as a loss, depression, grief, sadness, desperation, helplessness and hopelessness.
2) Anger including rage, frustration, powerlessness and feelings of injustice.
3) Anxiety consisting of fear, panic, stress, and tension.
4) Self blame including shame, feeling "contaminated", dirty and guilty.
5) Unreality with feelings of numbness, dead, unconnected and alienated.
6) Loneliness with fears of being separated, unsupported, a lack of contact, unheard and unloved.

The caregiver can be helpful to the resident with such feelings and emotions. The caregiver can:

1) Use supervision and group support to discuss problems.
2) Try to respond and not over-react.

3) Recognize powerful feelings, try to examine them and not deny or push them aside or out of his or her mind.

4) Ask questions about themselves, their feelings, and questions like:

   a) What is it about the resident's behavior that is frightening?

   b) What, if anything, do I bring to this experience from my past?

   c) What does being in control of oneself mean to me?

The caregiver may hold polarized opinions about various views of the resident. Part of the caregiver may want to agree with the resident while another part may want to reject him or her. The caregiver may feel repulsed or afraid. As a result, they should try to see the whole person, not just his or her injuries or scars of life. They should appreciate the resident's and his or her scars and accept the fact that they are there for a purpose and has helped the resident grow and survive as such things always generally assist the individual to learn from such experiences.

The caregiver may want to keep a list of times the resident has episodes of inappropriate behavior as a means of monitoring what the resident is feeling and find other channels for him or her to curtail their unacceptable behavior. In addition, the caregiver might withdraw his or her help if the resident's behavior is determined a symptom of their behavior, keeping in mind that inappropriate behavior is never rewarded.

Above all, the caregiver should make sure that they are providing services at a level, which they are trained to provide, and are comfortable within that they will be working with residents who have distressed and powerful feelings. It is vital for the caregiver to acknowledge their own feelings and limitations, and refer to someone who has the training, experience, and expertise necessary to deal with the problem or crises.

Residents express their emotions in different ways: anger, hostility, emotional pain, and sadness may be expressed overtly or as a "baseline." The resident may seem detached, sullen or depressed. The caregiver can easily be drawn into the resident's feelings of hopelessness or feel overextended by the resident's problems or feelings of inadequacy. In the counter-transference, the caregiver may feel weighed down or that they have to be all-powerful for the resident or one who nurtures. Nurturing can be useful, but a caregiver should be realistic about what they can offer, otherwise, they will be restricted by an unrealistic wish to fulfill all the resident's needs. For example, the caregiver probably cannot be with the distressed or psychotic resident for more than a few hours at a time due to the mental and emotional stress it places on the caregiver and, therefore, a network of support is needed for the resident. In this case, the caregiver can make sure that they and the resident have identified other available support systems. This could involve such key individuals as a nurse, social worker, psychologist, physician, or agency. Caregivers can prepare themselves for such demanding work with such residents by building an awareness of helping techniques, strategies, and interventions to give the resident a feeling of being therapeutically "held" and "comforted". Caregivers should also learn to take care of themselves when working with a resident with complex mental and emotional problems in addition to their physical needs. Adequate supervision is necessary for maintaining the quality of care it offers the caregiver. The supervisor will be aware of the potential impact of working with residents with high levels of distress. For example, a resident's grief may set off feelings of guilt and depression in the caregiver in relation to a past loss.

Some rules for the caregiver to encompass into their body of knowledge are as follows:

1) What one does as a caregiver matters.
2) Stay involved.
3) Adapt to your caregiving.
7) Set limits for one's self as well as the resident.
8) Foster learning, unlearning, and relearning skills.
9) Explain caregiving decisions made.
10) Never reward inappropriate behavior.

CHAPTER EIGHT

A CAREGIVER'S WORTH

Most caregivers who work as Certified Nursing Assistants question their worth and value. In describing their career, they use such words as "inferior, inadequate, fear, ill prepared, and a lack of respect." This is a momentous question, one on which much time has been invested by numerous people including the author. Although the job differs somewhat according to the policies and philosophies of different institutions, many basic parts of the job are inevitably the same. However, to most professional caregivers the feelings, attitudes, opinions and fears of this particular group of caregivers is understandable. Although real, it is something that only maturity, acquired knowledge and time will heal.

There are a number of factors, which contribute to this particular dilemma. For example, the men and women who fill this position do so with limited education and training. They are thrush into a job, which means that they will be working in close proximity with a variety of healthcare providers and specialists with formal education, and professional training, which far exceeds their own which threatens and over-whelms them. There are other factors. One thing with which this particular group of caregivers will have to cope is the all-important sameness of their job. It appears that every one of the residents is old, frail and sick with accompanying psychological and behavioral problems. Their job demands, first, then, that they must care for residents with this fact in mind. The second greatest part of the job is getting to know each resident—his or her name (or what they like to be called), their habits in relation to life's basic needs—eating, bathing, grooming, dressing, sleeping, elimination, medications and the outstanding indications of their behavior. The third major responsibility of their job lies in attempting to understand the resident. The reasons for certain behavior patterns are important. However, the residents for whom they are caring should be base lined so that the knowledge of these reasons can be used constructively in promoting recovery and lessening the possibilities of prolonging inappropriate behavior.

Further, attending staff conferences, ongoing in-service training and supervision, all of which are necessary, may result in undue anxieties. In all these tasks, they much learn to respect their co-workers, to work with them, to help the nurses in their special jobs, to keep the medical staff informed about the physical and psychological needs of the resident. All kinds of emergencies add to the job. Whatever the job, this group of caregivers if they are to be successful, should develop a healthy philosophy about his or her job and use it as the primary guide in caring for the residents. Although these and other factors may seem to be overwhelming to this group of caregivers, it also points to their importance and value.

The need for effective caregivers in our society is evident. As one travels around the nation, they cannot help but notice that scattered throughout the country, in every state, and county are facilities to care for our elderly population. There are countless nursing homes both large and small, special units to care for

Alzheimer's Dementia, psychiatric and behavior problems, assisted living facilities and group homes—the list goes on. They contain millions of beds for the elderly who are old, frail and sick. Many demonstrate different behaviors from the average, normal person. Because of their departure from the normal it has become necessary to place them in an environment which offers them numerous advantages--notably, security and understanding—and one in which their progress toward improved health can be accomplished more speedily. These facilities would not exist without caregivers who work as Certified Nursing Assistants. Again, this points to their value and importance.

For many years now, the bulk of the load of caring for these old and sick human beings has been the job of men and women who work as caregivers. Upon this group of caregivers has fallen the burden of daily, hourly contact with the very real and painful problems of living. There are insufficient numbers of personnel to adequately meet the complex needs of the elderly. This constitutes only one of the major problems of providing care for the elderly especially those experiencing dementia, Alzheimer's disease, psychiatric and behavior problems along with having to deal with the many dysfunctional families from which these individuals come. We as caregivers are acutely aware of two other factors, which places even more pressure on society and the healthcare system. They are: 1) the elderly residents desire to live and face death and dying issues at home, which places more emphasis on home care and less on institutional care, and 2) end of life issues, which places even more pressures on society and the caregiver.

However, progress has and is being made. During the past half century, tremendous strides have been made in the improvement of care for the elderly. Each year new facilities are being constructed, more mature and better trained caregivers are being recruited, new forms of care is being discovered and new steps are being made toward making the general public more aware of its obligations toward caring for the elderly and doing so in a more humane manner.

Furthermore, the philosophy of caring for the elderly is changing with more consideration being given to home care. Throughout all this runs the problem of status for the caregiving community. There is not enough professionals being trained by our colleges and universities, and the caregivers who provide basic hands-on care receive far less training than others on the staff in how to adequately care for the elderly. However, this need has not gone unnoticed. Foresighted, intelligent leaders have long recognized the courage, the service and the worthwhileness of this group of caregivers. They have known elderly individuals who have recovered and are quick to recognize the caregiver who helped the individual improve or get well; they have observed the lone caregiver who works performing tasks repeatedly which becomes discouraging; they have watched the caregiver lifting, bathing and changing an elderly resident and doing so with gentleness and humor. They have depended on the caregiver to help them with prescribed treatment processes, to watch over the residents at night and to comfort residents whose relatives have not come to visit. These things and many more have made recognition of the caregiver an actual fact and have prompted administrative personnel and lay leaders to campaign for better salaries, set up improved educational and training programs, to formulate better screening policies for hiring new caregivers and to consider the status of caregivers in relation to other professions in the community.

The question is often raised as to why anyone would want to

become a caregiver at this level and make it a career. Well, we who are caregivers ask ourselves the same question. Why would those of us who are professional caregivers spend our careers dealing with situations that would be a challenge to anyone? Many residents, for example, are from dysfunctional families. Yet we enter their domain going where angels dare to tread. We enter because we care. We are expected to have all the answers for dealing with residents from families who place their parents in nursing homes with a philosophy of "out of sight-out of mind", to bring some degree of security to replace the families' violence, neglect and abuse. Why would anyone want to exhibit such behavior?

Our answer, of course, is because we care. The most unique contribution we make in caring for the elderly is our closeness as caregivers. Our goal must be to provide the safest environment and help the resident achieve his or her highest level of habilitation possible. To achieve these goals the caregiver must first possess to some degree and understanding of the resident's medical, mental, social and spiritual problems, which require both maturity and training, formal and informal in nature. A caregiver is no longer a mere "sitter". We are much more than that, not only to the resident, but to the family and to other staff members as well. We are the ones who spend most time with the resident—hour-by-hour and minute by minute. We deal with behaviors, which are crucial, important, and essential to the resident's care. The role of the nursing home is changing and will continue to do so as well as the demand and role of the caregiver will continue to evolve. For example, the nursing home is becoming an extension of the hospital providing vital health care services once provided by the hospital industry. Therefore, it is essential that future caregivers be employed with a higher degree of training to ensure maximum effectiveness in understanding and providing the highest level of care as a caregiver to residents for which they are responsible.

Insufficient numbers of caregivers lacking adequate training constitute only one of the major problems of providing care to the elderly suffering from complicated problems including Alzheimer's dementia. In reality, if there were enough individuals adequately trained to provide highly specialized and intensified, personal care necessary to maintain the resident with Alzheimer's dementia, there would continue to exist economic barriers, which in many nursing homes cripple the caregiver in his or her job to the point of hopelessness. The caregiver works with the resident day in and day out, at times without instruction and guidance, often knowing if what he or she is doing is right, or wrong. There are times when we know that what we are doing could be done more efficiently. This is slowly changing, however, as federal and state regulations are and will continue to address both the standard care of residents residing in nursing homes and long-term care facilities. Each year new and innovative design of buildings are being constructed, more workers are being recruited, new methods of treatment discovered and new steps are being made toward educating the general public as to its obligations toward caring for the elderly especially those with Alzheimer's dementia.

Throughout all this runs the problem of the status of the caregiver. Farsighted and innovative leaders have long recognized the service and value of the caregiver's contributions. They have known of or had a relative who received care from a caregiver and observed first hand his or her duties and did so in a professional manner. However, on the other hand they have not been impressed by unkempt living areas where a lone caregiver toils all day at a discouraging task. They also have observed activities of daily living being addressed by caregivers as they lifted, bathed, and changed the elderly who was experiencing problems with their bodily functions and doing so with gentleness and humor. They have witnessed caregivers watching over their residents at night and comforting the residents whose family did not visit or participate in team meetings or a special event at the facility. These things and many other issues have made recognition and value of the caregiver an actual fact. For example, they have prompted the professional community, administrative, governmental and lay leaders to campaign for improved working conditions and salaries, and set up educational programs, to formulate better screening policies for hiring new workers for the rule of a caregiver and to consider the status and importance of the caregiver. In addition, relationships with other staff members began by integrating and accepting them as a vital member of the nursing care team. They begin to realize that the caregiver's constant contact with the resident and family members make them valuable to the treatment process as they know things about the resident—the physical, mental, emotional, spiritual and behavior of family members which is vital to the treatment team during the resident's habilitation.

The problems of the elderly has been around since human existence began as archeology excavations have revealed evidence about how earlier generations including prehistoric man dealt with the elderly. Probably, the first prehistoric tribes banished their elderly from their group, leaving them alone and at the mercy of storms, cold weather, wild beasts or starvation. In prehistoric times, the very preservation of life was man's major responsibility, and the elderly who could no longer contribute or care for him or herself was, out of necessity, cast out of the family and/or tribe.

As research progressed, the data revealed that the course of the elderly throughout the development of civilization was a complex one. Their journey reflected both the positive and negative aspects of the attitudes toward such suffering of the elderly. For example, during early Biblical times, temples were built in idyllic spots where special forms of treatment were provided, not unlike our present day therapeutic activities such as music therapy, hydrotherapy, occupational and physical therapy, and this period known as the "Golden Age" of Greece when this tolerant attitude towards the elderly prevailed.

However, with the downfall of these lavish early empires, attitudes also took a turn. For many hundreds of years, in fact, up until the middle of the 18th century, the elderly were treated without much worth or dignity. Medieval man looked upon the elderly especially those with dementia, as ones who were possessed by evil spirits, devils and demons, which must be driven from their bodies by the most drastic means. Only the religious orders offered assistance, but so few found their way into churches or monasteries that the unjust toll in human life among the elderly was appalling.

Conversely, our political leaders suddenly became aware of the potential power of the over sixty-five population and began to court their favor. Federal legislation had significant impact on the care of the elderly. Programs, which directly affected the areas of service, were developed and implemented which expanded governmental rules. In addition, quality control efforts are continuing to insure that additional concerns and problems are clarified. Homes for the elderly, public housing projects, medical institutions, recreational centers and communities that are devoted to the exclusive use of the retired have been increasing in number and in size in recent years. Retirement villages have been sponsored by philanthropic and private organizations, unions, church group and others. Even established communities, which are now known as retirement centers, have become inundated by older migrants seeking identification and special contiguity with "the clan".

During this time, Alzheimer's disease emerged from obscurity. Alzheimer's disease, named after Dr. Aloes Alzheimer, a German Neurologist who in 1906 studied the changes in the brain tissue of a woman who was one of his patients who died of an unusual mental illness. Once seen as a rare disorder, which was misunderstood, viewed and dreaded by many of the lay public as "old timer's disease", it is now seen by both the professional and lay public as a major public health problem that has a severe impact on millions of the elderly and their families.

Regardless of where the Alzheimer's resident is cared for, whether in the home, assisted living facilities, nursing homes, or special care units, the caregiver plays a vital role in the day-to-day care of the resident. Most facilities make every attempt to employ competent personnel who work as caregivers.

In today's healthcare facilites, most make every effort to employ competent personnel. They screen applicants to insure that they are of good character and possess certain characteristics and attitudes before he or she is accepted for employment. The salary, the prestige, and the interest of the job are more attractive, therefore, more and more individuals who have humane principals and are interested in healthcare and in their fellowman are being employed. They recognize sickness as such and want to do something about it. Urban facilities are employing more and more college and university students, both men and women. Everywhere, throughout the country, the input is more and more toward education for the caregiver, either in or on the job training, or the more formal educational programs pursuing degrees from community colleges in the helping professions.

Being an effective caregiver, in today's society, is or should be a proactive job. It is imperative that the caregiver improve his or knowledge base. The caregivers should take it upon themselves to pursue educational opportunities. They can do so by attending professional conferences, seminars and lectures at community colleges other than being dependent upon in-house in-service training and supervision. The caregiver can be proactive by:

- Educating ourselves
- Being assertive and innovative
- Recognizing human emotions of fear, anger and frustration
- Ignoring statistics (concentrate instead on care)
- Maintaining good mental, emotional and physical health
- Always be receptive to innovative methods of care
- Taking care of paperwork (if not documented, then it has not been done)
- Be receptive of treatment plans (goals, objectives, strategies, evaluations)
- Accepting concept of team approach and continuity of care
- Adhering to the concept of holistic care (treating the total person).

The future remains bright for the caregiver in today's society. The elderly needs a caregiver who will care about him or her, care for what happens, talk to them when they are unable to talk for themselves, who will help them learn or relearn all over again how to eat, sleep, groom, dress and toilet themselves. The resident needs to know that they will be with another human being who can accept him or herself for who they are.

It is this recognition of illness and inherent need of care that the caregiver must constantly keep uppermost in his or her mind during the caregiving process. As a caregiver who has logged in excess of forty years working with the elderly, I have found the physical, mental, emotional and behavioral issues to be extremely complex and challenging. The many problems I faced were like a giant octopus waiting to engulf me as I struggled to perform my daily duties.

As a caregiver, I am acutely aware and wish to impress those who are considering becoming a caregiver, out of choice or necessity, that caregiving is like life - "difficult". For some it will be a way of life while others will find the issues faced so complex and demanding that the complicated issues often evoke in us feelings of frustration, fear, grief, sadness, loneliness, guilt, anxiety, despair and even anger which can result in neglect, verbal and even physical aggression toward the resident for whom we are caring. It is no wonder that we as caregivers often become sick due to the stress involved requiring help for ourselves.

However, as we mature as a caregiver we find that difficult circumstances often reveal that we feel better when we spend our time helping others. It does not matter how bad our situation may seem, there is always others, in some manner, worse off than we are who need our assistance. These human emotional traits turn our pain into joy and our job as a caregiver into something meaningful and worthwhile. This book takes us the caregiver behind the scenes and forces us to examine the "who, when, what and how" in our residents as well as ourselves.

The most unique contribution, which is made by the caregiver, is providing effective quality care to the elderly, which in all cases is our closeness to the resident for whom we are caring. Throughout this text, it has been pointed out repeatedly that the courage, the hard work and the faithfulness of us as caregivers have been and will always be the mainstay of our profession in caring for the elderly entrusted to us for their care.

Not all caregivers fulfill this description; but the majority does. The author has no doubt that the future is bright and holds a prominent recognition for work he or she performs seeking but seldom asking for the recognition he or she so rightfully deserves. Listed below are some tips, which the author has found useful in achieving success as a caregiver. The author refers to the tips that have helped him as a caregiver as the "B" attitudes of caregiving. They are:

- Be positive.
- Be calm.
- Be caring.
- Be patient.
- Be confident.
- Be determined.
- Be assertive.
- Be creative.
- Be a good listener.
- Be a good communicator.
- Be able to exhibit a good attitude.
- Be receptive.
- Be optimistic.

In conclusion, caregiving is challenging. It consists of problems, depending upon their nature, which can and often evokes in us frustration, fear, grief, sadness, loneliness, guilt, anxiety, despair and even anger. However, on the other hand, there is worthwhileness in the art of caregiving. For example, we receive those human emotions of joy, fulfillness, and accomplishment giving our lives substance, meaning and relevance. It is by the Grace of God we come as a caregiver. However, after reading this book if you do not feel you have the personal or practical resources to take on caregiving responsibilities, then refrain from doing it. Acknowledging our limitations shows maturity, wisdom, and not weakness.

REFERENCES

Anderson, Ellis, and Marsha Dryan, (1988). Aging Parents and You: New York: Media Limited.

Appleton, William S., (2000z0. Prozac and the New Antidepressants: What you Need to Know. New York: Plume.

Baer, I., (2000). Getting Control Overcoming Your Obsessions and Compulsions, rev., ed. New York: Plume.

Berman, Claire, (2000). Caring for Yourself While Caring for Your Aging Parents. New York: Henry Holt.

Burler, Robert, (1975). Why Survive? Being Old in America. New York: Harper and Row.

Cameron, Julia, (1992). The Artist's Way: A Spiritual Path to Higher Creativity. New York: Jeremy P. Tarcher.

Carter, Rosalynn, (1989). Helping Yourself Help Others. New York: Times Books.

Clum, George A., (1990). Coping with Panic: A Drug Free Approach to Dealing with Anxiety Attacks. Pacific Grove, CA: Brooks/Cole.

Collett, M., (1997). Stay Close and Do Nothing: A Spiritual and Practical Guide to Caring for the Death and Dying at Home. Kansas City: Andrews McMeel Publishing.

Craske, M.G., and D. H. Barlow, (2000). Mastery of Your Anxiety and Panic, 3rd Ed. (MAP). San Antonio, TX: The Psychological Corporation.

Davidson, Jonathan, (2003). The Anxiety Book: Developing Strength in The Face of Fear. New York: Riverhead Books.

Davis, M.E.R. Eshelman and M. McKay, (1995). The Relaxation and Stress Reduction Workbook, 4th Ed. Oakland, CA: New Harbinger Publications.

Dossey, Larry, (1989). Recovering the Soul: A Scientific and Spiritual Search. New York: Bantam.

Eldridge, G. D., and J. R. Walker, (2000). Coping with Panic Workbook. VA: Self-Change Systems.

Eshelman, Davis M., and M. McKay, (1995). The Relaxation and Stress Reduction Workbook, 5th Ed. Oakland, CA: New Harbinger Publications.

Fanning, Patrick, (1988). Visualization for Change, Oakland, CA: New Harbinger Publishers.

Fineberg, Naomi, ed., (2001). Obsessive-Compulsive Disorder: A Practical Guide. London: Taylor and Francis.

Frankl, Viktor, (1998). Mans Search For Meaning. New York: Washington Square Press.

Gorman, Jack, (1992). The Essential Guide to Psychiatric Drugs. New York: St. Martin's Press.

Graedon, Teresa, and Joe Graedon, (1999). Deadly Drug Interactions: The People's Pharmacy Guide. New York: St. Martin's Press.

Greenburg, Vivian, (1989). Your Best is Good Enough: Aging Parents and Your Emotions. New York: Lexington Books.

Greenburg, Vivian, (1994). Children of a Certain Age: Adults and Their Aging Parents. New York: MacMillan.

Greenburg, Vivian, (1998). Respecting Your Limits When Caring for Aging Parents. Somerset, N.J.: Jossey-Bass.

Halpern, James, (1987). Helping Your Aging Parents: A Practical Guide for Adult Children. New York: Fawcett Crest.

Hartman, C., and J. S. Huffaker, (1995). The Fearless Flyer: How to Fly in Comfort and Without Trepidation. Portland, OR: Eighth Mountain Press.

Hope, D.A., R.C. Heimberg, H.R. Juster, and C.L. Turk, (2000). Managing Social Anxiety. San Antonio, TX: The Psychological Corporation.

Jacobsen, Edmund, (1974). Progressive Relaxation. Chicago: The University Press of Chicago, Midway Reprint.

Jamison, Kay Redfield, (1997). An Unquiet Mind. New York: Random House.

Jampolsky, Gerald, (1987). Good-Bye to Guilt. New York: Bantam Books.

Jeffers, Susan, (1987). Feel the Fear and Do It Anyway. San Diego, CA: Harcourt, Brace, Jovanovich.

Klein, Allen, (1989). Healing Power of Humor. Los Angeles: Tarcher.

Klein, D. F. and P. H. Wender, (1990). Do You Have a Depressive Illness? How to Tell, What to Do. New York: Harper Collins.

Klein, Donald F., and Anne Sheffield, (1999). How You Can Survive When They're Depressed: Living and Coping with Depression Fallout. New York: Crown.

Lebow, Grace, et al, (1999). Coping with Your Difficult Older Parent: A Guide for Stressed Out Children. New York: Harper Collins.

Levin, Norma Jean, (1997). How to Care for Your Parents: A Practical Guide to Eldercare. New York: W. W. Norton.

Llardo, Joseph A., (1998). As Parents Age. Acton, MA: Vanderwyk and Burnham.

Mace, Nancy I., and Peter V. Rabins, (1999). The 36 Hour Day: A Family Guide to Caring for Persons with Alzheimer's Disease, Related Dementing Illnesses, and Memory Loss in Later Life. Baltimore: Johns Hopkins University Press.

McLend, Beth W., (1999). Caregiving: The Spiritual Journey of Love, Loss, and Renewal. New York: John Wiley and Sons.

Moore, Thomas, (1994). Care of the Soul: A Guide for Cultivating Death and Sacredness in Everyday Life. New York: Harper Perennial.

Morris, V. Butler, (1996). How to Care for Aging Parents. New York: Workman Press.

Myres, Edward, (1997). When Parents Die. New York: Penguin.

Nuland, Sherwin B., (1999). How We Die. New York: Alford A. Knopf.

Opler, Lewis A., and Carol Bialkowski, (1994). Prozac and Other Psychiatric Drugs. New York: Pocket Books.

Paulson, Terry, (1989). Making Humor Work. Los Altos, CA: Crisp Publishing.

Penzel, F., (2000). Obsessive-Compulsive Disorders: Getting Well and Staying Well. New York: Oxford University Press.

Ripich, D., (2004). In It Together. Making Everyday Routines Easier for the Person with Alzheimer's disease. Forest Laboratories.

Towsend, M. C., (2000). Psychiatric Mental Health Nursing. Concepts of Nursing. Third Edition. Philadelphia: F. A. Davis Company.

Weil, Dr. Andrew, (1995). Spontaneous Healing. New York: Ballantine Books.

Zane, M. D., and H. Milt, (1984). Your Phobia: Understanding Your Fears Through Contextual Therapy. Washington, D. C.: American Psychiatric Press.

ABOUT THE AUTHOR

Dr. Ramage is a native of Mississippi and received his education in Southern Schools and Universities. He received his professional degrees and training from the Universities of Tennessee, Vanderbilt, Mississippi, North Carolina and Walden after receiving his undergraduate degrees from Itawamba Community College and Delta State University. Dr. Ramage is a Board Certified Fellow and Diplomate in Medical Psychotherapy and is a Board Certified Diplomate in Clinical Social Work. He also holds a Graduate Degree in Behavioral Psychology and practices as a behavioral therapist and consultant. He has extensive professional experience with programs for the elderly and their families serving the older population throughout the Southeast. Dr. Ramage has developed policy and behavioral intervention strategies for nursing home practitioners, administrators, educators and researchers in the area of dementia, Alzheimer's, behavioral and mental health issues in the elderly. He has published numerous articles on mental health issues in professional journals and has previously authored two books, "Creating Therapeutic Activity Plans in Long Term Care Facilities: The Basic Principles", and "A Caregiver's Training Manual for the Elderly." He was awarded an Honorary Degree, Doctor of Christian Humanities (D.C.H.) from Cambridge Theological

Seminary for his contributions in serving the elderly and more specifically his research in the areas of dementia and Alzheimer's Disease. Dr. Ramage resides with his wife, Margaret, in Northport, Alabama, where he maintains a private practice.

Made in the USA
Las Vegas, NV
02 March 2021